TINA TURNER

All The Top 40 Hits

Craig Halstead

Copyright © Craig Halstead 2020

All rights reserved. No part of this publication may be reproduced, stored in a retrieval system, or transmitted in any form or by any means, electronic, mechanical, photocopy, recording or otherwise, without prior written permission of the copyright owner. Nor can it be circulated in any form of binding or cover other than that in which it is published and without similar condition including this condition being imposed on a subsequent purchaser.

First Edition

for Aaron

BY THE SAME AUTHOR ...

Christmas Number Ones

This book details the Christmas No.1 singles in the UK from 1940 to date, and also reveals the Christmas No.2 single and Christmas No.1 album. The book also features the Christmas No.1s in five other countries, namely Australia, Germany, Ireland, the Netherlands and the USA, and is up-dated annually in January.

The 'All The Top 40 Hits' Series

This series documents, in chronological order, all the Top 40 Hit Singles and Albums by the featured artist:

ABBA
Annie Lennox
Blondie
Boney M.
Carpenters
Chi-Lites & Stylistics
Donna Summer
Janet Jackson
Michael Jackson
The Jacksons
(Jackson 5 / Jacksons / Jermaine / La Toya / Rebbie / 3T)
Olivia Newton-John
Whitney Houston

Top 40 Music Videos are also detailed in the three Jackson books.

The 'For The Record' Series

The books in this series are more comprehensive than the 'All The Top 40 Hits' volumes, and typically include: The Songs (release d & unreleased), The Albums, The Home Videos, The TV Shows/Films, The Concerts, Chartography & USA/UK Chart Runs, USA Discography & UK Discography.

Donna Summer
Janet Jackson
Michael Jackson
Whitney Houston

ACKNOWLEDGEMENTS

I would like to thank Chris Cadman, my former writing partner, for helping to make my writing dreams come true. It's incredible to think how far we have come, since we got together to compile 'The Complete Michael Jackson Discography 1972-1990', for Adrian Grant's *Off the Wall* fan magazine in 1990. Good luck with your future projects, I will look forward to reading them!

Chris Kimberley, it's hard to believe we have been corresponding and exchanging chart action for 30+ years! A big thank you, I will always value your friendship.

I would like to thank the online music community, who so readily share and exchange information at: Chartbusters (chartbusters.forumfree.it), ukmix (ukmix.org/forums), Haven (fatherandy2.proboards.com) & Buzzjack (buzzjack.com/forums). In particular, I would like to thank:

- 'BrainDamagell' & 'Wayne' for posting current Canadian charts on ukmix;
- 'flatdeejay' & 'ChartFreaky' for posting German chart action, and 'Indi' for answering my queries regarding Germany, on ukmix;
- 'mario' for posting Japanese chart action, and 'danavon' for answering my queries regarding Japan, on ukmix;
- 'Davidalic' for posting Spanish chart action on ukmix;
- 'Shakyfan', 'CZB', 'beatlened' & 'trebor' for posting Irish charts on ukmix;
- 'janjensen' for posting Danish singles charts from 1979 onwards on ukmix;
- 'Hanboo' for posting and up-dating on request full UK & USA chart runs on ukmix. R.I.P..

If you can fill any of the gaps in the chart information in this book, or have chart runs from a country not already featured in the book, I would love to hear from you. You can contact me via email at: **craig.halstead2@ntlworld.com** ~ thank you!

CONTENTS

INTRODUCTION	7
ALL THE TOP 40 SINGLES	17
THE ALMOST TOP 40 SINGLES	142
TINA'S TOP 40 SINGLES	144
SINGLES TRIVIA	149
ALL THE TOP 40 ALBUMS	161
THE ALMOST TOP 40 ALBUMS	244
TINA'S TOP 20 ALBUMS	245
ALBUMS TRIVIA	247

INTRODUCTION

Tina Turner, with a career spanning more than five decades, is one of the most successful singers and entertainers of all-time.

Tina, as Anna Mae Bullock, was born at Brownsville's Haywood Memorial Hospital on 26th November 1939. Her parents Zelma Priscilla (nee Currie) and Floyd Richard Bullock, who already had two daughters, Evelyn Juanita and Ruby Alline, soon took her to the family home in Nutbush, Tennessee. Anna was in her mid-teens when she learned Evelyn, together with two of her cousins, had died in a car crash.

After graduating from Sumner High School, St. Louis, in 1958, Anna found work as a nurse's aide at Barnes-Jewish Hospital. Even before she graduated, she and her sister Alline regularly went to R&B nightclubs in and around St. Louis, and it was at Club Manhattan where she first saw Ike Turner and his Kings of Rhythm perform. Alline started dating a member of the band, Eugene Washington.

Ike Turner, who was eight years older than Anna, had formed the Kings of Rhythm with three friends, Clayton Love, Eugene Fox and Raymond Hill, whilst they were still at high school. When Anna asked him if she could sing with them, Ike said he would contact her, but he never did.

'Finally one night I made my move,' revealed Tina, in her biography, *I Tina – My Life Story*. 'It was intermission and things were quiet. Most of the band had gone outside for some air, and Ike was up on stage by himself, just playing the organ.'

Ike was playing B.B. King's *You Know I Love You*, which was a song Anna knew.

'So I took the mike,' she said, 'and I started singing … and boy, Ike – that blew him away.'

Impressed by her voice, Ike allowed Anna to sing several more songs as the evening progressed, and invited her to sing with the Kings of Rhythm on a regular basis. Due to her skinny stature, Ike nicknamed her 'Little Ann'.

The following year, after a brief relationship with the band's saxophonist, Raymond Hill, Anna gave birth to a son, Craig. The same year, she received her first credit on a record, on the single *Boxtop*, which credited 'Ike Turner, Carlson Oliver & Little Ann'.

In 1960, quite by chance, Anna Mae Bullock became Tina Turner.

When Art Lassiter failed to turn up for a recording session, to sing a song titled *A Fool In Love*, which Ike has written specially for him, Ike turned to Anna.

'I had been there at the house when they were rehearsing the song,' said Tina, 'so I knew it. And Ike had already booked the studio time, so he said, "Little Ann, I want you to come and do this demo for Art".'

Ike planned to replace Anna's vocals just as soon as Lassiter showed. But, due to financial issues with Ike, Lassiter never did show.

'I don't know what Art Lassiter's argument with Ike was, 'said Tina. 'They fought a lot. Ike was always losing singers – he was very hard to work for.'

After hearing Anna and Ike's recording Henry 'Juggy' Murray, president of Sue Records, wanted to release it.

'Ike sent *A Fool In Love* to every record company in the country,' Murray revealed in *I Tina – My Life Story*', 'and every one of them turned it down. I didn't know him from a hole in the wall when the tape arrived in my office, but I knew it was a hit.'

Murray offered Ike a $25,000 advance for the song, and told Ike to forget re-recording it with a male vocal – it was Anna's voice that made the song.

Ike, without consulting Anna, accepted and credited the single to 'Ike & Tina Turner', his thinking being that if Anna left him as well, he could always replace her with another female singer.

A Fool For You, as well as giving her a new identity, gave Tina her first chart success. It rose to no.2 on Billboard's Soul chart, and achieved no.27 on the Hot 100.

A Fool Too Long came next, but it wasn't a hit. *I Idolize You* and *I'm Jealous* were both minor hits, before *It's Gonna Work Out Fine* gave Ike & Tina their biggest hit to date ~ it charted at no.14 on the Hot 100.

Tina and Ike had a son, Ronnie, who was born in October 1960, and went on to marry in Tijuana, Mexico, in 1962. By this time, Ike had already been married several times, and he brought two young sons ~ Ike, Jr. and Michael ~ he'd had with his common-law wife

Lorraine Taylor to the relationship. This meant, in the space of just a few years, Anna Mae Bullock had not only changed her name to Tina Turner, but she had gone from being single and childless to being a wife, mother and step-mother to four very young boys.

Ike & Tina Turner's musical career was hit and miss, but they did have some notable successes, including *River Deep – Mountain High*, *Proud Mary* and *Nutbush City Limits* (although Ike actually had nothing whatsoever to do with the recording of *River Deep – Mountain High*).

Tina has described her relationship with Ike as controlling and abusive, and even after they were married he continued to be promiscuous. 'In his mind, sex was power,' she said. 'When a woman became his conquest, he believed he owned her'.

Things became so bad, Tina attempted suicide in 1968, by taking an overdose of Valium (known today as Diazepam).

'Right after dinner,' she wrote in her autobiography, *My Love Story*, 'I took the pills, all fifty of them, which is not an easy thing to do.'

Rushed to the nearest hospital, Tina's stomach was pumped, and she survived.

'My suicide attempt wasn't a classic cry for attention, for help,' she stated. 'When I took those pills, I chose death, and I chose it honestly. I was unhappy when I woke up.'

Six years later, in July 1976, Tina and Ike flew to Dallas for a show. At the time, according to Tina, her husband was recovering from one of his five day cocaine benders, and was in a foul mood. Soon after they landed, he started on at Tina, but this time when Ike swore at her, she surprised him by swearing back at him. The row quickly escalated into a physical fight, which left both of them battered and bleeding. At the Statler Hotel, as soon as Ike fell asleep, Tina quickly gathered her bags together and did something she had wanted to do for a long, long time: she left her husband.

Tina and Ike were formally divorced in March 1978.

Between 1974 and 1979, Tina released four solo albums:

- *TINA TURNS THE COUNTRY ON!* (1974)
- *ACID QUEEN* (1975)
- *ROUGH* (1978)
- *LOVE EXPLOSION* (1979)

I, Tina

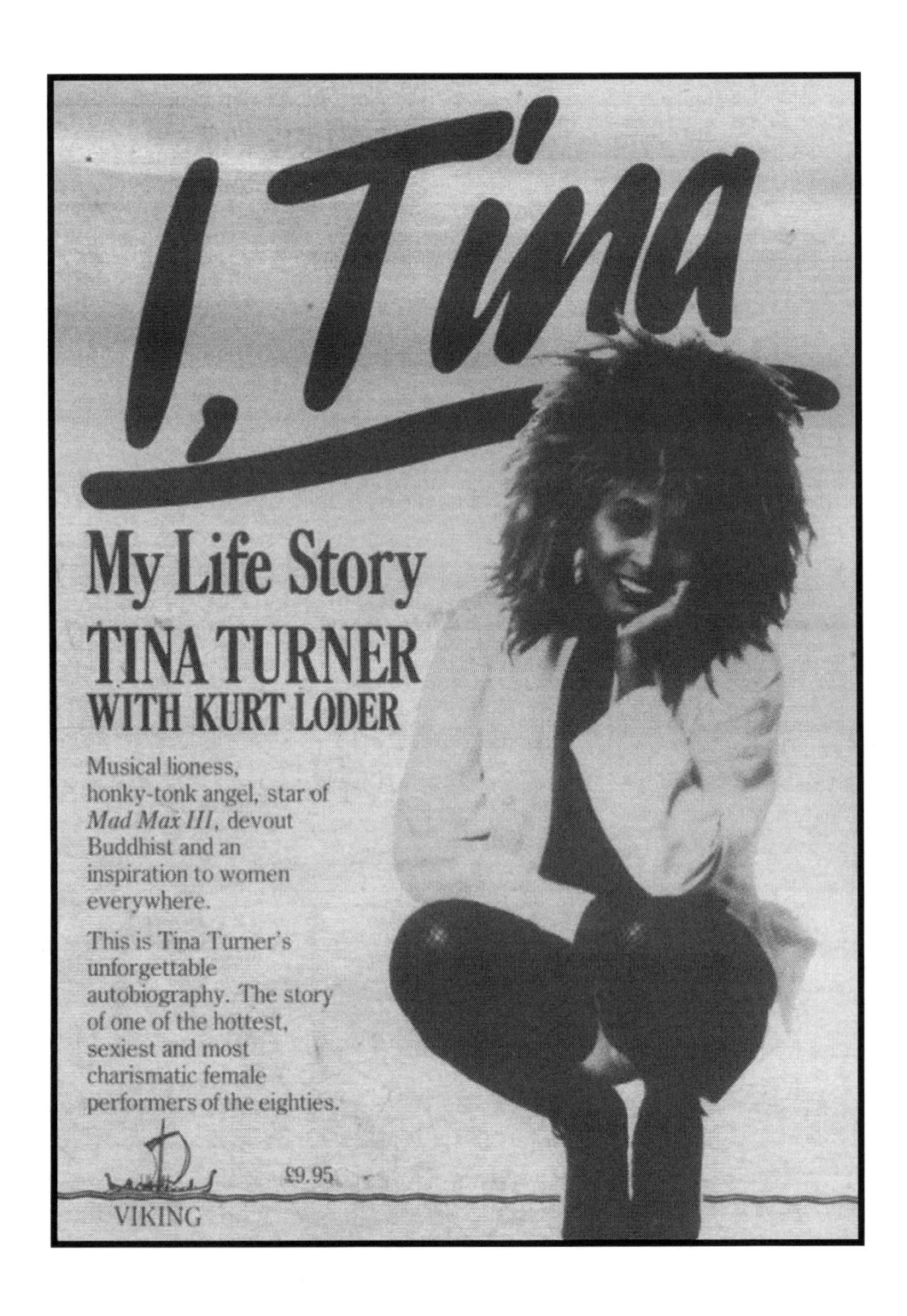

My Life Story
TINA TURNER
WITH KURT LODER

Musical lioness, honky-tonk angel, star of *Mad Max III*, devout Buddhist and an inspiration to women everywhere.

This is Tina Turner's unforgettable autobiography. The story of one of the hottest, sexiest and most charismatic female performers of the eighties.

£9.95

VIKING

ACID QUEEN was a minor no.115 hit on the Billboard 200 in the United States, but *TINA TURNS THE COUNTRY ON!*, *ROUGH* and *LOVE EXPLOSION* all failed to chart anywhere.

Tina's cover of the Temptations hit, *Ball Of Confusion (That's What The World Is Today)*, was a hit in Norway, but it wasn't until she covered Al Green's *Let's Stay Together* that Tina tasted international success as a solo artist. Her *PRIVATE DANCER* album, which featured *Let's Stay Together*, went on to become one of the best-selling albums of all-time by a female artist.

Often referred to as the Queen of Rock'n'Roll, Tina has sold 200+ million records worldwide. She has won eight Grammy Awards, three Grammy Hall of Fame Awards and a Grammy Lifetime Achievement Award. She was inducted into the Rock and Roll Hall of Fame, with Ike, in 1991.

Tina has appeared in more than a dozen films, most notably *Tommy* (1975), *Mad Max Beyond Thunderdome* (1985) and *Last Action Hero* (1993).

In 1986, with Kurt Loder, Tina published her memoir, *I, Tina – My Life Story*, in which she made public the brutal domestic abuse she had suffered at the hands of her husband Ike for the first time. Seven years later, the book was turned into a hugely successful film, *What's Love Got To Do With It*, in which Angela Bassett played Tina.

Tina: The Tina Turner Musical, which premiered at the Aldwych Theatre in London's West End on 17th April 2018, also told Tina's life story. The show opened on Broadway the following November.

Tina's autobiography, *My Love Story*, was published in 2018.

My Love Story

TINA TURNER

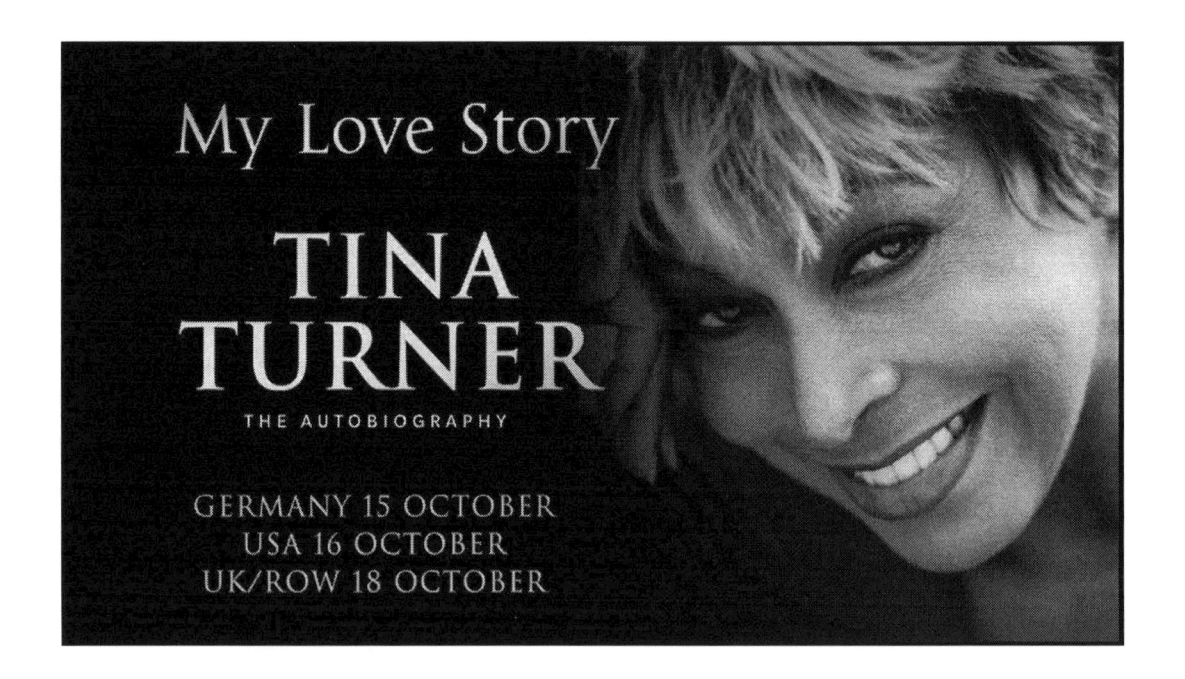

THE AUTOBIOGRAPHY

GERMANY 15 OCTOBER
USA 16 OCTOBER
UK/ROW 18 OCTOBER

All The Top 40 Hits

For the purposes of this book, to qualify as a Top 40 hit, a single or album must have entered the Top 40 singles/albums chart in at least one of the countries featured in this book: Australia, Austria, Belgium, Canada, Denmark, Finland, France, Germany, Ireland, Japan, the Netherlands, New Zealand, Norway, Spain, Sweden, Switzerland, the United Kingdom, the United States of America and Zimbabwe (formerly Rhodesia).

The Top 40 singles and albums are detailed chronologically, according to the date they first entered the Top 40 in one or more of the featured countries. Each Top 40 single and album is illustrated and the catalogue numbers and release dates are detailed, for both the United States and the UK, followed by the chart runs in each featured country, including any chart re-entries. Where full chart runs are unavailable, peak position and weeks on the chart are given.

For both singles and albums, the main listing is followed by 'The Almost Top 40 Singles/Albums', which gives an honorable mention to Tina's singles/albums that peaked between no.41 and no.50 in one or more countries. There is also a points-based list of Tina's Top 40 Singles and Top 20 Albums, plus a fascinating 'Trivia' section at the end of each section which looks at Tina's most successful singles and albums in each of the featured countries.

The Charts

The charts from an increasing number of countries are now freely available online, and for many countries it is possible to research weekly chart runs. Although this book focuses on

Top 40 hits, longer charts runs are included where available, up to the Top 100 for countries where a Top 100 or longer is published.

Nowadays, charts are compiled and published on a weekly basis – in the past, however, some countries published charts on a bi-weekly or monthly basis, and most charts listed far fewer titles than they do today. There follows a summary of the current charts from each country featured in this book, together with relevant online resources and chart books.

Australia
Current charts: Top 100 Singles & Top 100 Albums.
Online resources: current weekly Top 50 Singles & Albums, but no archive, at **ariacharts.com.au**; archive of complete weekly charts dating back to 2001 at **pandora.nla.gov.au/tep/23790**; searchable archive of Top 50 Singles & Albums dating back to 1988 at **australian-charts.com**.
Books: 'Australian Chart Book 1970-1992' & 'Australian Chart Book 1993-2009' by David Kent.

Austria
Current charts: Top 75 Singles & Top 75 Albums.
Online resources: current weekly charts and a searchable archive dating back to 1965 for singles and 1973 for albums at **austriancharts.at**.

Belgium
Current charts: Top 50 Singles & Top 200 Albums for two different regions, Flanders (the Dutch speaking north of the country) and Wallonia (the French speaking south).
Online resources: current weekly charts and a searchable archive dating back to 1956 for singles and 1995 for albums at **ultratop.be**.
Book: '*Het Belgisch Hitboek – 40 Jaar Hits In Vlaanderen*' by Robert Collin.
Note: the information in this book for Belgium relates to the Flanders region.

Canada
Current charts: Hot 100 Singles & Top 100 Albums.
Online resources: weekly charts and a searchable archive of weekly charts from the Nielsen SoundScan era at **billboard.com/biz** (subscription only); incomplete archive of weekly RPM charts dating back to 1964 for singles and 1967 for albums at **collectionscanada.gc.ca/rpm** (RPM folded in 2000).
Book: 'The Canadian Singles Chart Book 1975-1996' by Nanda Lwin.
Note: due to the patchy nature of the RPM archive, the information in this book relates to singles only, and is taken from Nanda Lwin's book

Finland
Current charts: Top 20 Singles & Top 50 Albums.
Online resources: current weekly charts and a searchable archive dating back to 1995 at **finnishcharts.com**.

France
Current charts: Top 200 Singles & Top 200 Albums.
Online resources: current weekly and archive charts dating back to 2001 can be found at **snepmusique.com**; a searchable archive dating back to 1984 for singles and 1997 for albums is at **lescharts.com**; searchable archive for earlier/other charts at **infodisc.fr**.
Book: '*Hit Parades 1950-1998*' by Daniel Lesueur.
Note: Compilation albums were excluded from the main chart until 2008, when a Top 200 Comprehensive chart was launched.

Germany
Current charts: Top 100 Singles & Top 100 Albums.
Online resources: current weekly and archive charts dating back to 1977 can be found at **offiziellecharts.de/charts**.
Books: '*Deutsche Chart Singles 1956-1980*', '*Deutsche Chart Singles 1981-90*' & '*Deutsche Chart Singles 1991-1995*' published by Taurus Press.

Ireland
Current charts: Top 100 Singles & Top 100 Albums.
Online resources: current weekly charts are published at IRMA (**irma.ie**); there is a searchable archive for Top 30 singles (entry date, peak position and week on chart only) at **irishcharts.ie**; an annual Irish Chart Thread has been published annually from 2007 to date, plus singles charts from 1967 to 1999 and album charts for 1993, 1995-6 and 1999, have been published at ukmix (**ukmix.org**); weekly album charts from March 2003 to date can be found at **acharts.us/ireland_albums_top_75**.
Note: the information presented in this book relates to singles only.

Italy
Current charts: Top 100 Singles & Top 100 Albums.
Online resources: weekly charts and a weekly chart archive dating back to 2005 at **fimi.it**; a searchable archive of Top 20 charts dating back to 2000 at **italiancharts.com**; pre-2000 information has been posted at ukmix (**ukmix.org**).
Books: *Musica e Dischi Borsa Singoli 1960-2019* & *Musica e Dischi Borsa Album 1964-2019* by Guido Racca.
Note: as the FIMI-Neilsen charts didn't start until 1995, the information detailed in this book is from the Musica & Dischi chart.

Japan
Current charts: Top 200 Singles & Top 300 Albums.
Online resources: current weekly charts (in Japanese) at **oricon.co.jp/rank**; selected information is available on the Japanese Chart/The Newest Charts and Japanese Chart/The Archives threads at **ukmix.org**.

Netherlands
Current charts: Top 100 Singles & Top 100 Albums.

Online resources: current weekly charts and a searchable archive dating back to 1956 for singles and 1969 for albums at **dutchcharts.nl**.

New Zealand
Current charts: Top 40 Singles & Top 40 Albums.
Online resources: current weekly charts and a searchable archive dating back to 1975 at **charts.org.nz**.
Book: 'The Complete New Zealand Music Charts 1966-2006' by Dean Scapolo.

Norway
Current charts: Top 20 Singles & Top 40 Albums.
Online resources: current weekly charts and a searchable archive dating back to 1958 for singles and 1967 for albums at **norwegiancharts.com**.

South Africa
Current charts: no official charts.
Online resources: none known.
Book: 'South Africa Chart Book' by Christopher Kimberley.
Notes: the singles chart was discontinued in early 1989, as singles were no longer being manufactured in significant numbers. The albums chart only commenced in December 1981, and was discontinued in 1995, following re-structuring of the South African Broadcasting Corporation.

Spain
Current charts: Top 50 Singles & Top 100 Albums.
Online resources: current weekly charts and a searchable archive dating back to 2005 at **spanishcharts.com**.
Book: *'Sólo éxitos 1959-2002 Año a Año'* by Fernando Salaverri.

Sweden
Current charts: Top 60 Singles & Top 100 Albums.
Online resources: current weekly charts and a searchable archive dating back to 1975 at **swedishcharts.com**.
Note: before 1975, a weekly Top 20 *Kvällstoppen* charts was published, which was a sales-based, mixed singles/albums chart.

Switzerland
Current charts: Top 75 Singles & Top 100 Albums.
Online resources: current weekly charts and a searchable archive dating back to 1968 for singles and 1983 for albums at **hitparade.ch**.

UK
Current Charts: Top 100 Singles & Top 200 Albums.

Online resources: current weekly Top 100 charts and a searchable archive (Top 40s only) dating back to 1960 at **officialcharts.com**; weekly charts are posted on a number of music forums, including ukmix (**ukmix.org**), Haven (**fatherandy2.proboards.com**) and Buzzjack (**buzzjack.com**).

Note: weekly Top 200 album charts are only available via subscription from UK ChartsPlus (**ukchartsplus.co.uk**); weekly Top 200 singles are no longer published anywhere.

USA

Current charts: Hot 100 Singles & Billboard 200 Albums.

Online resources: current and archive weekly charts are available at **billboard.com**; weekly charts are also posted on a number of music forums, including ukmix (**ukmix.org**), Haven (**fatherandy2.proboards.com**) and Buzzjack (**buzzjack.com**).

Note: older 'catalog' albums (i.e. albums older than two years) were excluded from the Billboard 200 before December 2009, so the chart didn't accurately reflect the country's best-selling albums. Therefore, in this book Billboard's Top Comprehensive Albums chart has been used from December 2003 to December 2009, as this did include all albums. In December 2009 the Top Comprehensive Albums chart became the Billboard 200, and Billboard launched a new Top Current Albums chart – effectively, the old Billboard 200.

Zimbabwe

Current charts: no official charts, and no known online resources.

Books: 'Zimbabwe Singles Chart Book' & 'Zimbabwe Albums Chart Book' by Christopher Kimberley.

Note: Zimbabwe was, of course, known as Rhodesia before 1980, but the country is referred to by its present name throughout this book.

Note: In the past, there was often one or more weeks over Christmas and New Year when no new album chart was published in some countries. In such cases, the previous week's chart has been used to complete a chart run. Similarly, where a bi-weekly or monthly chart was in place, for chart runs these are counted at two and four weeks, respectively.

All The Top 40 Singles

1 ~ A Fool In Love

USA: Sue Records 730 (1960).
   B-side: *The Way You Love Me*.

29.08.60: 87-67-47-49-44-40-30-**27**-40-34-33-56-62

UK: London Records 45-HLU 9226 (1960).
   B-side: *The Way You Love Me*.

A Fool In Love wasn't a hit in the UK.

Ike Turner wrote *A Fool In Love* for Art Lassiter, who was a vocalist with his Kings of Rhythm band. The song was scheduled to be recorded at the Technisonic Studios in St. Louis, Missouri, in March 1960, by Lassiter and The Artettes, a vocal trio comprising Frances Hodges, Robbie Montgomery and Sandra Harding. However, while The Artettes turned up for the recording session, Lassiter was a no-show.

   Anna Mae Bullock, who had been nicknamed 'Little Ann' by Ike due to her skinny build, knew the song from rehearsals, and was keen to take Lassiter's place. Having booked and paid for the studio, Ike agreed she could record *A Fool In Love* as a demo, intending to replace her vocals with Lassiter's at the earliest opportunity.

   It later transpired, due to financial disputes with Ike, Lassiter had quit the Kings of Rhythm. Then, when a local DJ heard *A Fool In Love*, he suggested Ike send it to Juggy Murray, president of New York's Sue Records. Ike did so and, hearing a potential hit, Murray offered Ike a $25,000 advance for the song.

Ike accepted, and he changed Ann's name to 'Tina Turner'; at the same time, fearful she might do a Lassiter and quit as well, he trademarked the name, thinking if she did leave he could always replace her with another singer.

So the duo Ike & Tina Turner was born.

A Fool In Love rose to no.2 on Billboard's Soul chart, and crossed over to the pop chart, peaking at no.27 on the Hot 100. The duo's debut single went on to sell over a million copies in the United States alone, but it wasn't a hit anywhere else.

A Fool In Love was included on Ike & Tina's debut album, *THE SOUL OF IKE & TINA TURNER*, released in early 1961, but unlike the single the album failed to chart.

Ike & Tina re-recorded *A Fool In Love,* for their 1966 album, *RIVER DEEP – MOUNTAIN HIGH.*

2 ~ It's Gonna Work Out Fine

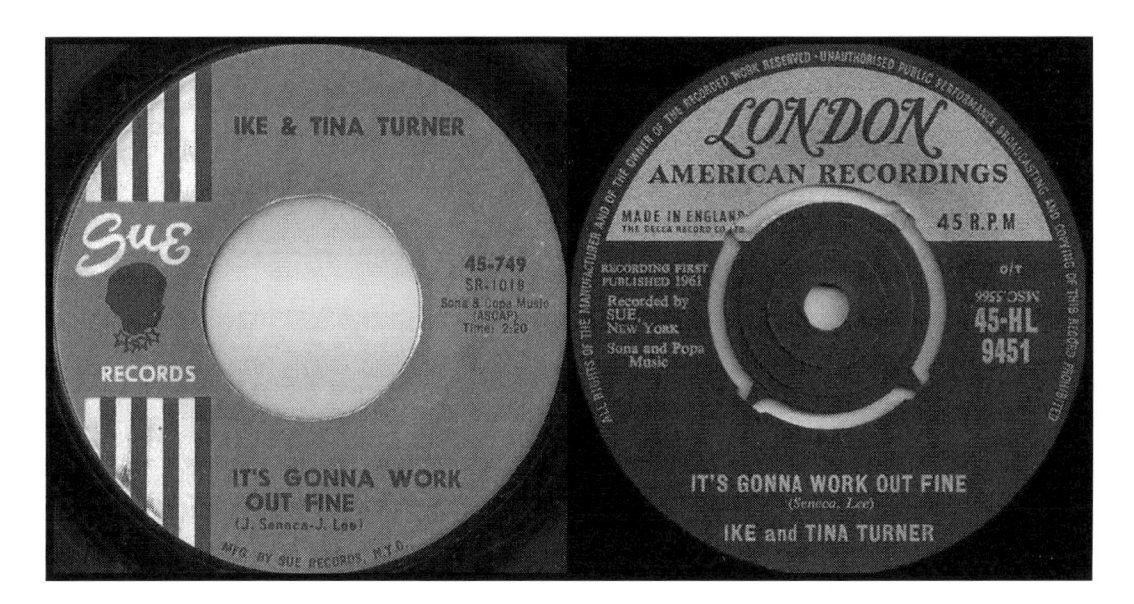

USA: Sue Records 45- 749 (1961).
B-side: *Won't You Forgive Me.*

31.07.61: 76-74-64-56-42-38-31-**14**-18-35-55-49-47-56-74

UK: London Records 45-HL 9451 (1961).
B-side: *Won't You Forgive Me.*

It's Gonna Work Out Fine wasn't a hit in the UK.

It's Gonna Work Out Fine was composed by Rose Marie McCoy and Joe Seneca (*aka* Sylvia McKinney). The song was brought to Ike & Tina's attention by McCoy, and although Juggy Murray was credited with producing their recording of the song, Mickey Baker and Sylvia Robinson of the duo Mickey & Sylvia were also involved.
 'I paid for the session, taught Tina the song,' Robinson confirmed, 'that's me playing guitar.'
 Like *A Fool In Love*, *It's Gonna Work Out Fine* rose to no.2 on Billboard's Soul chart, and it gave Ike & Tina their biggest hit yet on the Hot 100, peaking at no.14. However, like *A Fool In Love*, the single wasn't a hit anywhere outside the United States.
 It's Gonna Work Out Fine became Ike & Tina's second million seller, and won them their first Grammy nomination, for Best Rock & Roll Recording. The award, however, went to Chubby Checker's *Let Twist Again*.
 It's Gonna Work Out Fine was included on two early Ike & Tina albums, 1962's *DYNAMITE!* and 1963'a *IT'S GONNA WORK OUT FINE*.

Ike & Tina re-recorded *It's Gonna Work Out Fine* for their 1966 album, *RIVER DEEP – MOUNTAIN HIGH*, and in 1993 Tina re-recorded the song for the soundtrack of her biopic, *WHAT'S LOVE GOT TO DO WITH IT*, with her saxophonist Timmy Cappello singing Ike's lines.

The duo Mickey & Sylvia recorded *It's Gonna Work Out Fine* in 1960, however, their version remained unreleased until it was included on their 1990 compilation, *LOVE IS STRANGE*.

3 ~ Poor Fool

USA: Sue Records 45-753 (1961).
  B-side: *You Can't Blame Me*.

27.11.61: 95-73-58-47-46
6.01.62: 42-39-43-**38**-44-58

UK: Not Released.

Poor Fool was written by Ike, and was recorded by Ike & Tina for their 1962 album, *DYNAMITE!*
   Released as the follow-up to *It's Gonna Work Out Fine*, *Poor Fool* gave the duo their third Top 40 success on Billboard's Hot 100, peaking at no.38. *Poor Fool* was also a no.4 hit on the Soul chart but, like Ike & Tina's previous singles, it failed to chart anywhere outside the United States.
   In common with *It's Gonna Work Out Fine*, *Poor Fool* also featured on Ike & Tina's 1963 album, *IT'S GONNA WORK OUT FINE*.

4 ~ River Deep – Mountain High

USA: Philles Records 131 (1966).
  B-side: *I'll Keep You Happy*.

28.05.66: 98-94-93-**88**

UK: London Records HLU 10046 (1966).
  B-side: *I'll Keep You Happy*.

9.06.66: 33-12-8-4-**3-3**-4-9-11-18-31-35-44
12.02.69: 45-39-33-44-45-45-48

Netherlands
9.07.66: 11-10-**9**-11-12

Spain
23.01.67: peaked at no.**10**, charted for 7 weeks

Although *River Deep – Mountain High* credited Ike & Tina Turner, it was actually Tina's first solo single, as Ike had no input whatsoever to the recording.
  The song was composed by Phil Spector, Jeff Barry and Ellie Greenwich.
  'I can't describe how special I felt,' wrote Tina in her autobiography, *My Love Story*, 'when Phil Spector, the legendary record producer, contacted Ike about wanting to work with me.'
  There was just one problem: Phil Spector wanted to work with Tina, but he didn't want to work with Ike.

'Phil was smart,' Tina wrote. 'He wanted no part of Ike or the trouble that came with him. Just Tina. Phil insisted that I came along to his house in Hollywood so we could start working on the song together.'

To make it happen, Phil Spector agreed to pay Ike $20,000. Ike insisted the payment be made in advance, which is what happened.

Tina recorded *River Deep – Mountain High* at the Gold Star studio, Los Angeles. Naturally, she started singing the song as she would have with Ike: full-on and very, very loud. But Phil Spector quickly stopped her, and said, 'No, no, not like that – just the melody.'

Tina couldn't believe her luck.

'I feel it even now,' she wrote in her autobiography, 'how exhilarating it was to be given permission to use my voice in a new way. I wanted to run and jump in the air and shout "Woo hoo!".'

River Deep – Mountain High gave Tina her biggest hit to date, especially in the UK, where the single spent two weeks at no.3. The single also achieved no. 9 in the Netherlands and no.10 in Spain.

However, it was a different story in Tina's homeland, where *River Deep – Mountain High* struggled to no.88, before it dropped off the Hot 100.

Tina explained the lack of success in the United States by saying: 'The deejays were puzzled about how to play it; if pressed, they said it wasn't 'black' enough to be rhythm and blues, or 'white' enough to be pop.'

Consequently, Ike & Tina's *RIVER DEEP – MOUNTAIN HIGH* album was cancelled in the United States, and wasn't released – with some changes – until three years later. At the same time, *River Deep – Mountain High* was reissued, and became a hit all over again in the UK, where second time around it peaked at no.33.

5 ~ A Love Like Yours

USA: Philles Records 136 (1967).
B-side: *I Idolize You*.

A Love Like Yours wasn't a hit in the USA.

UK: London Records HLU 10083 (1966).
B-side: *Hold On Baby*.

27.10.66: 38-32-26-21-**16**-17-18-28-33-43

A Love Like Yours (Don't Come Knocking Everyday) was composed by Motown's Holland-Dozier-Holland, and was originally recorded by Martha & The Vandellas ~ it was released as the B-side of Martha & The Vandellas' 1963 hit, *Heat Wave*.

Ike & Tina recorded *A Love Like Yours* for their 1966 album, *RIVER DEEP – MOUNTAIN HIGH*.

A Love Like Yours wasn't a hit in the United States, but it became Ike & Tina's second hit single in the UK where, riding the success of *River Deep – Mountain High*, it rose to no.16 on the chart.

6 ~ I Want To Take You Higher

USA: Liberty 56177 (1970).
  B-side: *Contact High*.

23.05.70: 78-68-63-60-59-57-56-53-53-52-47-38-37-35-**34-34**-37-44

UK: Liberty LBF 15367 (1970).
  B-side: *Contact High*.

I Want To Take You Higher wasn't a hit in the UK.

I Want To Take You Higher was written by Sly Stone, and was originally recorded by Sly & The Family Stone for their 1969 album, *STAND!*

Sly & The Family Stone released *I Want To Take You Higher* as the B-side of their single, *Stand!* ~ however, in early 1970 the two sides were flipped, and *I Wanted to Take You Higher* rose to no.38 on the Hot 100 in the United States.

Ike & Tina recorded a cover of *I Want To Take You Higher* for their 1970 album, *COME TOGETHER*, which was credited to Ike & Tina Turner and The Ikettes.

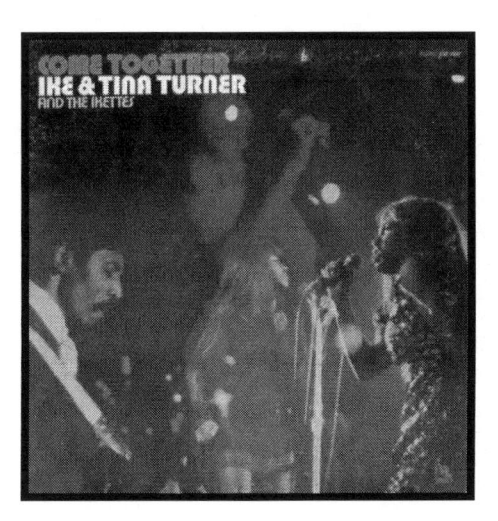

Released as a single just a few months after Sly & The Family Stone's version charted, Ike & Tina took *I Want To Take You Higher* to no.34 on the Hot 100 in the United States ~ four places higher than the original version achieved. However, *I Want To Take You Higher* wasn't a hit anywhere outside the United States.

7 ~ Proud Mary

USA: Liberty 56216 (1971), Virgin Records V25H-38434 (1993).
B-side (1971): *Funkier Than A Mosquita's Tweeter*.
Tracks (1993): *Proud Mary (Edit Live Version)/(Edit)/We Don't Need Another Hero (Live)/The Best (Live)*.

30.01.71: 99-63-37-32-21-12-7-6-**4**-6-9-11-23

UK: Liberty LBF 15432 (1970), Parlophone CDRDJ 6387 (1994).
B-side (1970): *Funkier Than A Mosquita's Tweeter*.
Tracks (1994): *Proud Mary (Radio Edit)/What's Love Got To Do With It/Disco Inferno/Proud Mary*.

2.10.10: **62**

Belgium
20.03.71: 25-17-**16-16-16**-20-21-27

Germany
15.03.71: 50-x-x-27-50-33-**21**-35-26-27-25-30-31-44-46-x-42

Netherlands
6.03.71: 19-16-14-12-12-13-10-9-7-10-6-**5**-7-10-15-24

Spain
7.06.71: peaked at no.**28**, charted for 2 weeks

Proud Mary was composed by John Fogerty in just two days, following his discharge from the National Guard, and was originally recorded by Creedence Clearwater Revival for their 1969 album, *BAYOU COUNTRY*.

Released as a single, Creedence Clearwater Revival scored a major hit with *Proud Mary*, charting at no.1 in Austria, no.2 in Canada and the United States, no.3 in New Zealand, no.4 in Germany, no.5 in Australia, no.6 in Norway, no.7 in Belgium, and no.8 in the Netherlands and the UK.

'I heard the Creedence Clearwater Revival song by John Fogerty and suggested doing our own version,' revealed Tina in her autobiography, *My Love Story*. 'Ike and I played around with it for a while – we did that with new material – but I didn't know if, or when, we would actually do it on stage. Ike kept those decisions to himself.'

Ike wasn't impressed with Creedence Clearwater Revival's version of *Proud Mary*, but he was interested in a cover by The Checkmates Ltd. featuring Sonny Charles, which was a minor no.69 hit in the United States.

Ike & Tina recorded *Proud Mary*, rearranged by Ike and Soko Richardson, for their 1970 album, *WORKIN' TOGETHER*.

'I loved the Creedence version,' said Tina, 'but I liked ours better after we got it down, with the talking and all. I thought it was more rock 'n' roll.'

As a single, *Proud Mary* rose to no.4 in the United States, no.5 in the Netherlands, no.16 in Belgium, no.21 in Germany and no.28 in Spain, but it failed to chart in the UK.

Ike & Tina invariably included *Proud Mary* in their live shows, and live versions of the song featured on two 1971 albums, *WHAT YOU HEAR IS WHAT YOU GET – LIVE AT CARNEGIE HALL* and *LIVE IN PARIS*.

Tina continued to perform *Proud Mary* live, after her split with Ike, and solo live versions were released on 1988's *LIVE IN EUROPE* and 2009's *TINA LIVE*.

Tina re-recorded *Proud Mary* for her 1993 soundtrack album, *WHAT'S LOVE GOT TO DO WITH IT*. This solo version was issued as a promotional single in some countries, but it wasn't a hit.

Proud Mary finally charted in the UK in October 2010, albeit for a single week at no.62, after one of the contestants performed the song on the hugely popular TV show, *The X Factor*.

Tina performed *Proud Mary* with Beyoncé at the 50th Annual Grammy Awards, staged at the Staples Center, Los Angeles, on 10th February 2008.

8 ~ Nutbush City Limits

USA: United Artists Records UA-XW298-W (1973).
  B-side: *Help Him*.

8.09.73: 89-78-61-50-47-44-41-36-30-24-**22**-23-38-41-48

UK: United Artists Records UP 35582 (1973), Capitol Records CL 630 (1991).
  B-side (1973): *Help Him*, B-side (1991): *The Best (Edit)*.

8.09.73: 47-32-18-8-5-**4**-**4**-9-16-27-32-46-47
21.09.91: 31-23-23-30-60 (The 90's Version)

Australia
3.12.73: peaked at no.**14**, charted for 52 weeks
28.10.91: peaked at no.**14**, charted for 15 weeks (The 90's Version)

Austria
15.12.73: 2-2-**1**-5-17 (monthly)
17.11.91: 30-x-25-30-30-30 (The 90's Version)

Belgium
16.09.78: 19-23-23-28
19.10.91: 33-21-21-18-16-**12**-22-24-26 (The 90's Version)

Germany
29.10.73: 30-21-27-11-12-9-6-7-4-7-7-**2**-4-3-**2**-6-4-8-9-12-13-14-17-40-28-42

By Public Demand
Entering NUTBUSH City Limits
IKE & TINA TURNER
'NUTBUSH CITY LIMITS'
B SIDE
HELP HIM
From the Album
'NUTBUSH CITY LIMITS'
Leaving NUTBUSH City Limits
First 15,000 available in picture bag
also Limited edition as 12" single
in picture bag

28.03.88: 48-49-53-45-50-64 (Live)
30.09.91: 98-81-25-29-27-28-32-32-37-46-85-100 (The 90's Version)

Ireland
25.10.73: 18
21.09.91: 18-**12**-13-28 (The 90's Version)

Italy
20.04.74: peaked at no.**7**, charted for 14 weeks
21.09.91: peaked at no.8, charted for 13 weeks (The 90's Version)

Netherlands
26.08.78: 18-16-**12-12-12**-21-20-27
12.10.91: 95-71-39-27-22-16-15-21-29-36-49-78 (The 90's Version)

New Zealand
17.02.74: peaked at no.**19**, charted for 2 weeks
3.11.91: 50-40-29-36-26-44-34 (The 90's Version)

Spain
29.04.74: peaked at no.**19**, charted for 4 weeks
2.05.88: peaked at no.29, charted for 6 weeks (Live)

Switzerland
5.12.73: 9-6-**2-2-2-2-2-2-2**-3-3-4-4-3-6-7-9-8
3.11.91: 22-x-12-18-12-17-28-20 (The 90's Version)

Zimbabwe
23.02.74: peaked at no.**1** (2), charted for 20 weeks

Tina wrote the semi-autobiographical *Nutbush City Limits* herself, and it gave Tina her first taste of success as a songwriter.

Ike & Tina recorded *Nutbush City Limits* at Ike's Bolic Sound studio in Inglewood, California. Among the session musicians who contributed to the recording, if his girlfriend at the time Gloria Jones is to be believed, was T. Rex's Marc Bolan, who Jones ~ who worked as a backing vocalist for Ike & Tina in the 1960s ~ asserted played guitar on the track.

Nutbush City Limits lent its title to Ike & Tina's 1973 album, and as a single it hit no.1 in Austria and Zimbabwe, and charted at no.2 in Germany and Switzerland, no.4 in the UK, no.7 in Italy, no.12 in the Netherlands, no.14 in Australia, no.18 in Ireland, no.19 in Belgium, New Zealand and Spain and no.22 in the United States.

A live version of *Nutbush City Limits*, recorded during Tina's Break Every Rule Tour, featured on her 1988 album, *LIVE IN EUROPE*. Released as the lead single, to promote the album, the live version achieved no.29 in Spain and no.45 in Germany, but it failed to chart in most countries.

Tina re-recorded *Nutbush City Limits*, in a more modern dance style, for her 1991 compilation album, *SIMPLY THE BEST*. Known as 'The 90s Version', this proved more successful than the live version had been, and took *Nutbush City Limits* into the charts again in many countries. The 90s Version charted at no.8 in Italy, no.12 in Belgium, Ireland and Switzerland, no.14 in Australia, no.15 in the Netherlands, no.23 in the UK, no.25 in Austria and Germany and no.26 in New Zealand.

Numerous artists have covered *Nutbush City Limits* over the years, including Bob Segar & The Silver Bullet Band, Precious Wilson & La Mama, Pseudo Echo and Sam Brown.

9 ~ Sexy Ida (Part 1)

USA: United Artists Records UA-XW528-X (1974).
  B-side: *Sexy Ida (Part 2)*.

2.11.74: 90-85-80-74-74-**65**-87-78

UK: United Artists Records UP 35726 (1974).
  B-side: *Sexy Ida (Part 2)*.

Sexy Ida wasn't a hit in the UK.

Italy
21.12.74: **25**

Spain
17.11.75: peaked at no.**25**, charted for 2 weeks

Like *Nutbush City Limits*, *Sexy Ida* was written by Tina, and was recorded at Ike's Bolic Sound studio. And, like *Nutbush City Limits*, it's claimed Marc Bolan was one of the session musicians who played on the recording.
  For single release, the track was split in two, with the more up-tempo second half of the song on the B-side.
  Sexy Ida (Part 1) couldn't match the success of *Nutbush City Limits*, but it did chart at no.25 in Italy and Spain, and no.65 in the United States.

10 ~ Baby – Get It On

USA: United Artists Records UA-XW598-X (1975).
  B-side: *Baby – Get It On (Disco Version)*.

7.06.75: 98-94-92-**88**

UK: United Artists Records UP 35766 (1975).
  B-side: *Baby, Get It On*.

5.07.75: b-b5-**b4**-b9-b8 (chart breaker)

Belgium
27.09.75: 24-**20**-26

Netherlands
16.08.75: 26-16-16-13-11-**9**-14
18.11.78: 30-27-34-41

Variously titled *Baby – Get It On*, *Baby, Get It On* and *Baby, Baby, Get It On*, this song was composed by Ike and, unusually for Ike & Tina recordings, Ike also sang lead vocals on the track. Once again, the session musicians playing on the recording are rumoured to include Marc Bolan.

Baby – Get It On was recorded at two studios, Ike's Bolic Sound and Dierks Studio in Stommein, Germany, as Ike & Tina were touring Europe at the time.

Although recorded by Ike & Tina, *Baby – Get It On* was released on Tina's second solo album, *ACID QUEEN*, released in 1975.

Given *ACID QUEEN* was a solo album by Tina, and Ike sang lead vocals on *Baby – Get It On*, releasing *Baby – Get It On* as the album's lead single was a curious choice. Nevertheless, the single charted at no.9 in the Netherlands and no.20 in Belgium, but it struggled to no.88 in the United States and spent five weeks as a 'chart breaker' in the UK, but failed to enter the Top 50.

Baby – Get It On was the duo's last Top 40 success, before Ike and Tina split, and Tina went her own separate way.

11 ~ Ball Of Confusion

USA: Not Released.

UK: Virgin Records VS 500 (1982).
   B-side: *Ball Of Confusion (Instrumental)*.

Ball Of Confusion wasn't a hit in the UK.

Norway
12.06.82: 9-8-7-**5**-8-10

Ball Of Confusion (That's What The World Is Today) was written by Norman Whitfield and Barrett Strong, and was originally recorded by the Temptations in April 1970 at Motown's Studio A, Hitsville USA in Detroit, Michigan ~ they took the song to no.2 in the United States and no.7 in the UK.

Tina recorded a cover of *Ball Of Confusion* for the 1982 album, *MUSIC OF QUALITY AND DISTINCTION VOLUME ONE*, which was a tribute album by the B.E.F. (British Electric Foundation), featuring members of Heaven 17 and Love & Rockets, plus guest vocalists covering hits from the 1960s and 1970s.

As well as Tina's version of *Ball Of Confusion*, the album also included:

- *There's A Ghost In My House* by Paul Jones.
- *These Boots Are Made For Walking* by Paula Yates.
- *Suspicious Minds* by Gary Glitter.
- *Wichita Lineman* by Glenn Gregory.
- *Anyone Who Had A Heart* by Sandie Shaw.

The album charted at no.25 in the UK, but it wasn't released in North America.

Tina's cover of *Ball Of Confusion* was a no.5 hit in Norway, but it didn't chart anywhere else. However, the recording did bring her to the attention of Capitol Records, who took a chance and signed her.

With Heaven 17's Ian Craig Marsh and Martyn Ware, Tina recorded another cover ~ Al Green's *Let's Stay Together* ~ and scored a surprise hit that finally kick-started her career as a solo artist.

12 ~ Let's Stay Together

USA: Capitol Records B-5322 (1984).
  B-side: *I Wrote A Letter*.

21.01.84: 72-59-46-43-38-34-30-30-27-**26**-31-44-62-76-92

UK: Capitol Records CL 316 (1983).
  B-side: *I Wrote A Letter*.

19.11.83: 36-16-7-**6-6**-9-9-12-17-27-37-43-68

Australia
16.01.84: peaked at no.**19**, charted for 18 weeks

Belgium
31.12.83: 35-23-23-12-8-**7-7**-17-32

Canada
19.03.84: peaked at no.**40**, charted for 3 weeks

Germany
2.01.84: 48-37-24-20-20-**18**-23-27-33-32-40-53-59-75-70

Ireland
4.12.83: 22-17-**15**-22-22-20-26

Let's Stay Together
Words and Music by WILLIE MITCHELL, AL GREEN AND AL JACKSON
Recorded by
Tina Turner
ON CAPITOL RECORDS
BURLINGTON MUSIC CO LTD.
DISTRIBUTED BY IMP

Netherlands
24.12.83: 23-7-11-**5**-9-14-17-23-38

New Zealand
5.02.84: 45-31-25-9-**4**-5-**4**-6-**4**-10-9-16-16-27-36-40-42

Switzerland
19.02.84: **28**

Let's Stay Together was written by Al Green, Willie Mitchell and Al Jackson, Jr, and was a no.1 hit for Al Green in the United States in 1971. His recording also charted at no.7 in the UK and no.14 in Canada, and lent its name to his 1972 album.

Having recorded *Ball Of Confusion* for the B.E.F. project, Tina went on to record a cover of *Let's Stay Together* with the same team.

'When I recorded *Let's Stay together*,' she said, 'I had a crush on someone back in America, so I did it as a love song. That's why my version was so different from Al Green's ... as I finished the last lyric, Martyn (Ware) called it a wrap. We got it done in one take.'

Roger Davies, Tina's manager, concurred. 'Tina walked in and sang *Let's Stay Together* live, in one take,' he said. 'It just happened. I got shivers down my back. These guys couldn't believe it. Tina said, "Let's do it again, I'm just getting warmed up." And they're going, "No, no – we'll keep this!" They went ahead and added all their little bits and pieces to it, and that take became the single.'

Since her split with Ike, Tina had found the going tough, but *Let's Stay Together* finally kick-started her solo career ~ but not, initially, in the United States where Capitol Records didn't rate the single and refused to release it. Only after the single had become a hit in Europe, and import copies were flooding the country, did Capitol Records realise their mistake, and finally rush-released the single.

Let's Stay Together gave Tina a surprise hit around the world, charting at no.4 in New Zealand, no.5 in the Netherlands, no.6 in the UK, no.7 in Belgium, no.15 in Ireland, no.18 in Germany, no.19 in Australia, no.26 in the United States, no.28 in Switzerland and no.40 in Canada.

Let's Stay Together was issued as a 12" picture disc in the UK.

Let's Stay Together has been recorded by numerous artists over the years, including Al Jarreau, Billy Paul, Boyz II Men, Craig David, Donny Osmond, Isaac Hayes, Maroon 5, Michael Bolton, Roberta Flack and Shirley Bassey.

13 ~ Help

USA: Not Released.

UK: Capitol Records CL 325 (1984).
  B-side: *Rock 'N' Roll Widow*.

25.02.84: 54-49-**40-40-40**-47

Belgium
3.03.84: 33-32-26-**25**-27-38

Netherlands
3.03.84: 33-23-18-**14**-24-40-49

Help! was written by John Lennon & Paul McCartney, and was recorded by the Beatles for their 1965 film and soundtrack album with the same title.
    As a single, the Beatles took *Help!* to no.1 in a host of countries, including Australia, Canada, Ireland, the Netherlands, New Zealand, Norway, Sweden, the UK and the United States.

Tina recorded a cover of *Help* (minus the exclamation mark), as a ballad, with the Crusaders. Her version was included on the European ~ but not North American ~ release of her *PRIVATE DANCER* album, and was released as the follow-up to *Let's Stay Together* in Europe.

Help was a modest success for Tina, charting at no.14 in the Netherlands, no.25 in Belgium and no.40 in the UK. The single was issued as a 7" picture disc in the UK only.

A live version of *Help* featured on Tina's 1988 album, *LIVE IN EUROPE*.

Other artists to have covered *Help!* include Bananarama with French & Saunders and Kathy Burke (as a charity single in support of Comic Relief), Carpenters, Deep Purple and John Farnham.

14 ~ What's Love Got To Do With It

USA: Capitol Records B-5354 (1984).
  B-side: *Rock And Roll Widow*.

19.05.84: 92-77-71-57-45-35-31-27-23-16-9-5-4-2-2-**1-1-1**-4-6-13-15-29-44-54-66-78-91

UK: Capitol Records CL 334 (1984).
  B-side: *Don't Rush The Good Things*.

16.06.84: 66-50-40-18-10-6-5-5-**3**-5-8-12-19-27-40-48

Australia
23.07.84: peaked at no.**1** (1), charted for 22 weeks

Austria
15.10.84: **4-4**-8-13-17-20 (bi-weekly)

Belgium
6.10.84: 37-27-25-**20**-24

Canada
1.10.84: peaked at no.**1** (1), charted for 18 weeks

France
3.11.84: **21**-24-23-**21**-22-22-27-26-28-30-31-22-33-42-45-49

Germany
6.08.84: 46-32-19-17-15-11-14-12-10-9-**7**-8-10-13-16-20-24-24-35-53-59-59-65-69

Ireland
15.07.84: 14-7-**4**-5-7-5-7-22-27

Italy
15.12.84: peaked at no.**16**, charted for 5 weeks

Netherlands
23.06.84: 38-46
8.09.84: 25-20-12-**10**-13-17-26-34-38

New Zealand
8.07.84: 37-26-**3-3-3-3**-5-5-5-10-9-13-24-21-29-31-30-38-44

Norway
17.11.84: **10**

South Africa
15.09.84: peaked at no.**2**, charted for 19 weeks

Spain
24.12.84: peaked at no.**8**, charted for 9 weeks

Sweden
28.09.84: 15-6-**4-4**-5-12 (bi-weekly)

Switzerland
5.08.84: 19-24-21-16-12-13-9-**8**-11-14-15-16-17-24-28-29-30

Zimbabwe
24.11.84: peaked at no.**2**, charted for 11 weeks

What's Love Got To Do With It was composed by Terry Britten and Graham Lyle, and was originally offered to Cliff Richard, who wasn't interested. Next, the song was offered to Donna Summer, but she never recorded it.

'I had *What's Love Got To Do With* It for two years,' Donna confirmed, in a 1999 interview, 'and I didn't do it. I realised after hearing what Tina did with it that had I sung the song it would never have sounded that way. Her raspiness, and the sensitivity of the song, is what made the match.'

Tina Turner

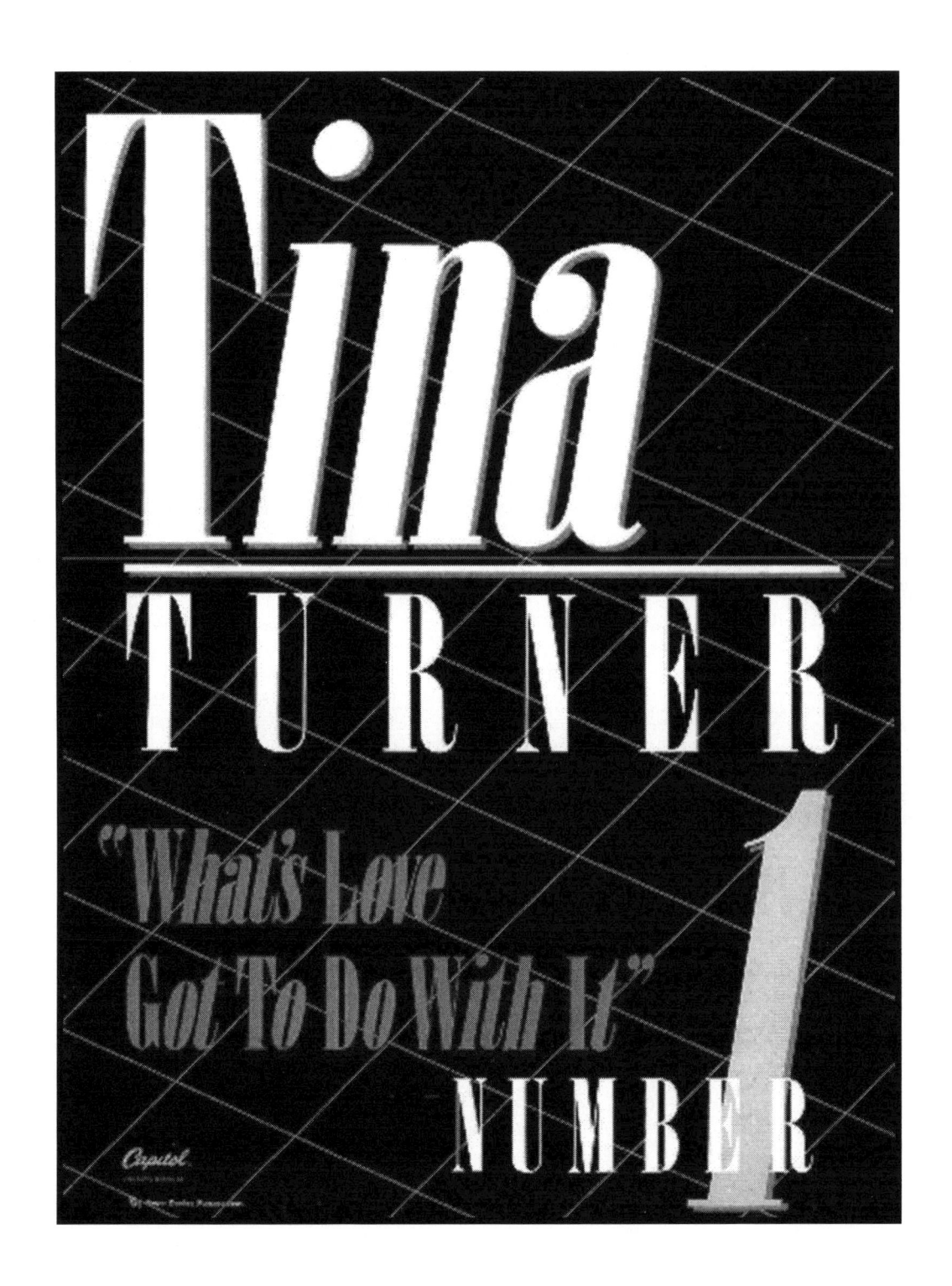

"What's Love Got To Do With It"

NUMBER 1

Capitol

Next in line were Bucks Fizz, with member Jay Ashton keen to sing lead on the track. However, the group's producer didn't think the song was suitable for a female lead, so when Bucks Fizz did record the song, they did so with lead vocals by male member Bobby G. Bucks Fizz planned to include *What's Love Got To Do With It* on their *I HEAR TALK* album, but shelved it after Tina's got her version out first, and it became a huge hit. Bucks Fizz's version remained unreleased until 2000, when it featured as a bonus track on their reissued album, *ARE YOU READY*.

Tina didn't want to record *What's Love Got To Do With It*.

'Roger (Davies) brought me a demo of *What's Love Got To Do With It*,' she revealed in her autobiography, *My Love Story*, 'and we immediately clashed because I didn't like the song, not one bit.'

Her manager did like the song; he thought it would be a huge hit.

Tina shared her concerns with Terry Britten, who as well as co-writing the song was going to produce Tina's version, and he listened.

'Then I decided to show him some respect,' said Tina. 'I sang his words, but I did it my way … forcefully, with gravity and raw emotion.'

Roger Davies was correct: *What's Love Got To Do With It* was huge. It gave Tina her first ~ and what proved to be her only ~ no.1 single in her homeland. The single also topped the chart in Australia and Canada, and achieved no.2 in South Africa and Zimbabwe, no.3 in New Zealand and the UK, no.4 in Austria, Ireland and Sweden, no.7 in Germany, no.8 in Spain and Switzerland, no.10 in the Netherlands and Norway, no.16 in Italy, no.20 in Belgium and no.21 in France.

THE HOT 100
Week of September 1, 1984

		THIS WEEK	LAST WEEK	PEAK	DURATION
1 ↑ +1	**What's Love Got To Do With It** Tina Turner	2	1		16
2 ↑ +3	**Missing You** John Waite	5	2		11
3 →	**Stuck On You** Lionel Richie	3	3		11
4 ↓ -3	**Ghostbusters** Ray Parker Jr.	1	1		12

What's Love Got To Do With It was issued as a 12" picture disc single in the UK, and went on to become the no.2 best-selling single of 1984 in the United States.

What's Love Got To Do With It won three Grammy Awards:

- Record of the Year
- Song of the Year
- Best Pop Vocal Performance, Female

What's Love Got To Do With It was inducted in the Grammy Hall of Fame in 2012.

15 ~ Better Be Good To Me

USA: Capitol Records B-5387 (1984).
B-side: *When I Was Young*.

15.09.84: 63-52-42-34-28-23-16-9-7-7-**5**-**5**-12-20-29-29-58-65-72-91-97

UK: Capitol Records CL 338 (1984).
B-side: *When I Was Young*.

15.09.84: 56-48-46-**45**-53

Australia
15.10.84: peaked at no.**28**, charted for 18 weeks

Belgium
5.01.85: **33**-34

Canada
19.11.84: peaked at no.**8**, charted for 11 weeks

Germany
28.01.85: **52**-55-61-67-65

Ireland
16.09.84: 27-**21**

Netherlands
12.01.85: 48-24-**22**-29-30-28-49

New Zealand
14.10.84: 27-**22**-26-32-30-42

Better Be Good To Me was written by Holly Knight, Nicky Chinn and Mike Chapman, and was originally recorded in 1981 by Spider, a band from New York City ~ co-writer Holly Knight was a member of Spider.

Tina recorded *Better Bo Good To Me* for her *PRIVATE DANCER* album, and it was released as the follow-up to *Help* in Europe, and to *What's Love Got To Do With It* in North America.

Better Be Good To Me charted at no.5 in the United States, no.8 in Canada, no.21 in Ireland, no.22 in the Netherlands and New Zealand, no.28 in Australia, no.33 in Belgium, no.45 in the UK and no.52 in Germany.

Better Be Good To Me was issued as a shaped 7" picture disc in the UK.

Tina won another Grammy Award for *Better Be Good To Me*, for Best Rock Vocal Performance, Female.

16 ~ Private Dancer

USA: Capitol Records B-5433 (1984).
  B-side: *Nutbush City Limits (Live)*.

19.01.85: 58-40-35-30-25-18-16-15-9-**7-7**-16-24-44-64-67-80-98

UK: Capitol Records CL 343 (1984).
  B-side: *Nutbush City Limits (Live)*.

17.11.84: 56-32-31-**26**-30-35-37-42-50

Australia
17.12.84: peaked at no.**21**, charted for 15 weeks

Belgium
10.11.84: 12-7-**5-5**-6-12-22-36

Germany
22.10.84: 71-30-32-24-22-22-**20**-22-28-33-33-46-49-66-71

Ireland
25.11.84: 19-**14**-15-x-29-29-29

Netherlands
20.10.84: 22-5-**4**-6-7-7-9-14-18-24-34-42

TINA TURNER

THE NEW SINGLE
Private Dancer

FROM THE
PLATINUM ALBUM & TAPE
'PRIVATE DANCER'
(TINA 1 & TC – TINA 1)
COMPOSED BY MARK KNOPFLER
OF DIRE STRAITS

12 inch full length version features
'RIVER DEEP MOUNTAIN HIGH'
& 'NUTBUSH CITY LIMITS'
Recorded LIVE in Chicago
earlier this year.

7 inch features
'NUTBUSH CITY LIMITS'
Recorded LIVE in Chicago
earlier this year.

Capitol Records

New Zealand
27.01.85: 10-**5**-6-7-8-23-22-26-45-41

Spain
6.05.85: peaked at no.**6**, charted for 21 weeks

Private Dancer was written by Mark Knopfler of Dire Straits.

'He'd written it for himself,' said Tina, 'but hadn't used it on his most recent album because he decided it was a song that was better for a woman than a man. He was absolutely right.'

The song is about prostitution.

'I have never had to stoop to that in my life,' said Tina, 'but I think most of us have been in situations where we had to sell ourselves, one way or another.'

Tina has admitted she was thinking about her relationship with Ike when she recorded *Private Dancer*: keeping quiet to avoid an argument, and staying with him when all she really wanted to do was leave him. Consequently, she found the whole recording process very emotional.

Legal issues meant the backing track that Dire Straits had recorded for *Private Dancer* couldn't be used by Tina, and Jeff Beck was drafted in to play guitar on her version in place of Mark Knopfler ~ a decision which Knopfler felt ruined the song.

Private Dancer, which lent its name to Tina's first successful album as a solo artist, continued her run of success. It achieved no. 4 in the Netherlands, no.5 in Belgium and New Zealand, no.6 in Spain, no.7 in the United States, no.14 in Ireland, no.20 in Germany, no.21 in Australia and no.26 in the UK.

17 ~ Tonight

USA: EMI America B-8246 (1984).
  B-side: *Tumble & Twirl* (David Bowie).

1.12.84: 74-62-**53**

UK: EMI America EA 187 (1984), Capitol Records 006-20 3179 7 (1988).
  B-side: *Tumble & Twirl* (David Bowie, 1984), *River Deep – Mountain High (Live)* (1988).

8.12.84: 58-**53**-59-64-x-x-94

Australia
17.12.84: peaked at no.**70**, charted for 9 weeks

Belgium
7.01.89: 34-24-18-9-4-4-4-4-**3**-5-9-12-22-37 (Live)

Germany
13.03.89: 41-45-45-**39**-55-69-74

Netherlands
15.12.84: 45
10.12.88: 70-43-30-17-4-2-2-**1-1**-2-2-8-10-20-29-38-57-100 (Live)

New Zealand
2.12.84: 37-28-**21-21-21-21-21**-23-38-50-48

Switzerland
6.01.85: 23-28-27-30
26.03.89: 29-**17**-26-24-29 (Live)

Tonight was written by David Bowie and Iggy Pop, and it was originally recorded by the latter for his 1977 album, *LUST FOR LIFE*.

Seven years later, David Bowie recorded *Tonight* himself as a duet with Tina, for his album with the same title. The duet was recorded a month or so after Tina's Grammy successes, and she has admitted, 'I still get goose bumps when I think about it.'

The collaboration led to Tina and David Bowie developing a special friendship, helped by the fact that Bowie, like her, was a Buddhist.

When *Tonight* was released as a single, only David Bowie was credited. The single charted at no.21 in New Zealand, no.23 in Switzerland, no.45 in the Netherlands, and no.53 in the United States and the UK.

On 23rd March 1985, David Bowie joined Tina live on stage at the NEC Arena in Birmingham, England, to perform *Tonight*. Three years later, this live recording was included on Tina's album, *LIVE IN EUROPE*.

The live version of *Tonight* hit no.1 in the Netherlands, and charted at no.3 in Belgium, no.17 in Switzerland and no.39 in Germany.

Tina Turner

NEW 7 INCH AND 12 INCH SINGLE

"I Can't Stand The Rain"

12 INCH FEATURES EXTENDED RE-MIX
B/W "LETS PRETEND WE'RE MARRIED"
RECORDED LIVE IN CHICAGO AUGUST '84

FEATURED ON THE PLATINUM ALBUM & TAPE
"PRIVATE DANCER"

Capitol

18 ~ I Can't Stand The Rain

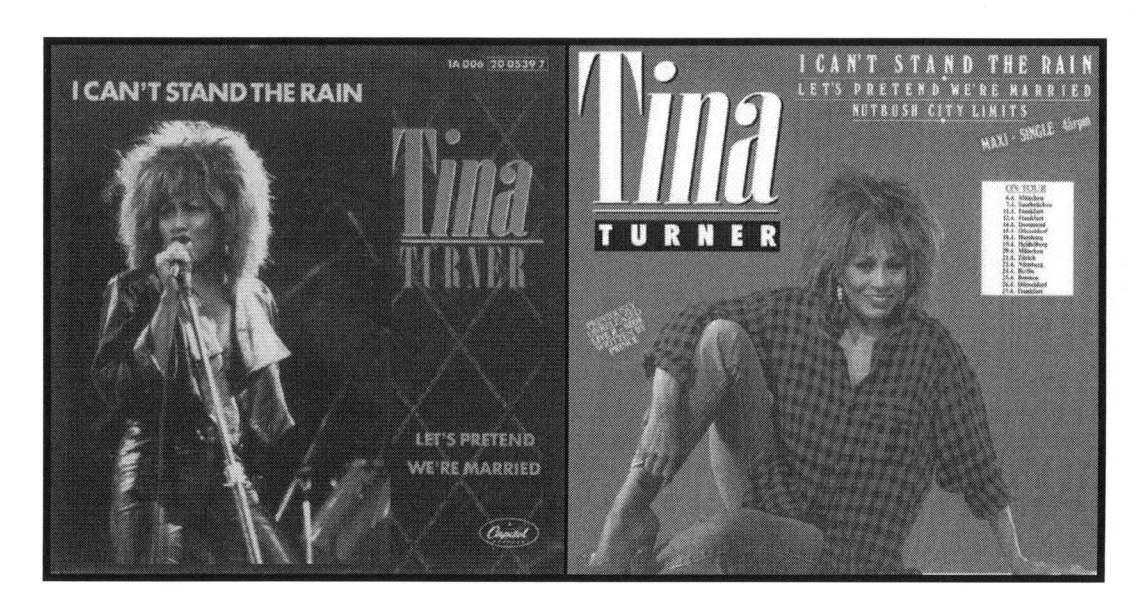

USA: Not Released.

UK: Capitol Records CL 352 (1985).
  B-side: *Let's Pretend We're Married.*

2.03.85: 74-**57**-64

Austria
1.05.85: 10-10-7-**6**-7-24 (bi-weekly)

Germany
22.04.85: 33-28-15-12-**9**-12-12-21-27-33-41-54-71-x-74

Ireland
2.03.85: 24-**20**

Switzerland
5.05.85: 29-23-18-**15**-16-20-19-20-30-25

I Can't Stand The Rain was written by Ann Peebles, Bernard 'Bernie' Miller and Don Bryant, and it was originally recorded by Ann Peebles for her 1974 album with the same title.
  As a single, Ann Peebles took *I Can't Stand The Rain* to no.38 in the United States and no.41 in the UK.

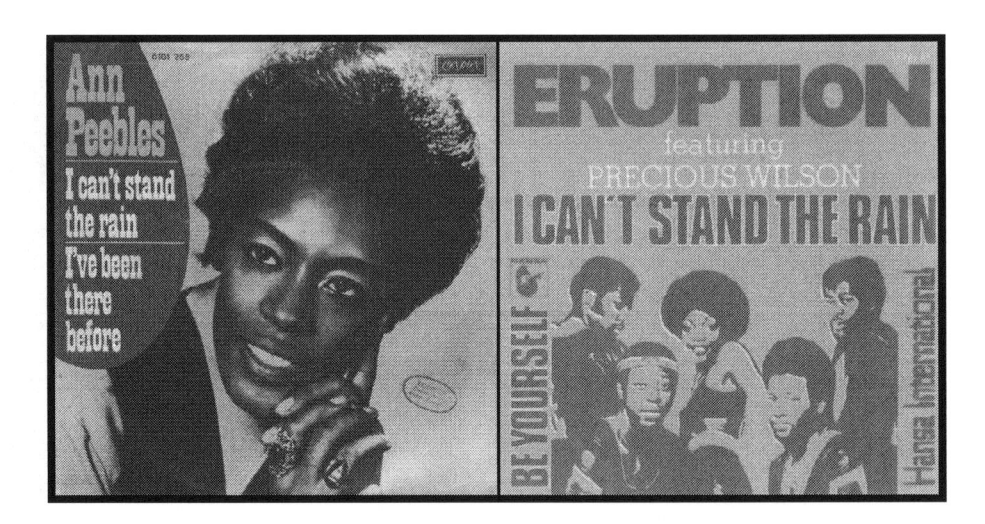

Eruption featuring Precious Wilson recorded a disco version of *I Can't Stand The Rain* in 1978, which proved more popular than the original recording, hitting no.1 in Australia and Belgium, and going Top 10 in a host of other countries, including Austria, France, Germany, Ireland, Italy, the Netherlands, New Zealand, Norway, South Africa, Switzerland and the UK.

Tina recorded a cover of *I Can't Stand The Rain* for her *PRIVATE DANCER* album. Outside North America, it was released as the sixth single from the album, and considering how many people had already bought the album it did well to chart at no.6 in Austria, no.9 in Germany, no.15 in Switzerland, no.20 in Ireland and no.57 in the UK.

We Are The World

USA: Columbia US7-04839 (March 1985).
  B-side: *Grace* (Quincy Jones).

23.03.85: 21-5-2-**1-1-1-1**-2-8-14-24-29-44-68-75-81-92-100

UK: CBS USAID 1 (April 1985).
  B-side: *Grace* (Quincy Jones).

13.04.85: 7-**1-1**-2-5-17-33-45-67
18.07.09: 77

Australia
1.04.85: peaked at no.**1** (9 weeks), charted for 26 weeks

Austria
15.04.85: 13-13-**2-2-2-2-2-2**-3-3-5-5-7-7-11-11-15-15

Belgium
30.03.85: 22-15-6-2-**1-1-1-1-1-1**-5-6-13-17-23-36-37

Canada
6.05.85: peaked at no.**3**, charted for 13 weeks

Finland
04.85: **1-1**-5-11 (monthly chart)

France
20.04.85: 20-11-**1-1-1**-2-2-2-2-2-3-5-7-10-12-14-16-13-21-22-31-50

Germany
8.04.85: 64-14-3-**2-2-2**-3-3-5-11-15-23-28-27-27-42-29-36-39-52-60

Ireland
14.04.85: **1-1-1-1**-2-3-8-29

Netherlands
30.03.85: 11-**1-1-1-1-1-1-1-1-1**-5-8-16-18-45-50
11.07.09: 64-50
29.12.18: 97

New Zealand
7.04.85: 4-**1-1-1-1-1-1-1-1**-4-8-21-29-34-x-45

Norway
23.03.85: 4-**1-1-1-1-1-1-1-1-1-1**-3-7-10-8-10-x-14

Spain
4.05.84: 10-2-**1-1-1-1-1-1-1-1**-3-2-2-4-3-3-5-?-7-14-14-16-20-22-24-26-?

Sweden
5.04.85: **1-1-1-1-1-1-1-1**-2-2-2-2-7-7-8-813-13-17-17

Switzerland
7.04.85: 12-6-2-2-**1-1-1-1-1-1**-3-6-7-9-11-14-15-23-21
12.07.09: 11-6-6
11.10.09: 98
29.11.09: 67-81-96
14.03.10: 64-x-72-x-75

Zimbabwe
11.05.85: peaked at no.**1** (7 weeks), charted for 24 weeks.

We Are The World was written by Michael Jackson and Lionel Richie, as America's answer to Band Aid's *Do They Know It's Christmas*. It was recorded by USA For Africa, with 'USA' standing for 'United Support of Artists', to aid famine relief in Ethiopia.

Stevie Wonder was originally approached to write the song, but he was in New York, and unable to make it. Michael and Lionel completed the lyrics to the song on 21st January 1985, and the track was largely recorded ~ with some minor changes to the lyrics ~ immediately after the American Music Awards ceremony in Hollywood, on 28th January.

The line 'we're taking our lives, in our own hands' was changed to 'we're saving our own lives', to avoid it being taken as a suicide line.

Tina was one of the soloists on *We Are The World*.

They were, in order of appearance on the record: Lionel Richie, Stevie Wonder, Paul Simon, Kenny Rogers, James Ingram, Tina Turner, Billy Joel, Michael Jackson, Diana Ross, Dionne Warwick, Willie Nelson, Al Jarreau, Bruce Springsteen, Kenny Loggins, Steve Perry, Daryl Hall, Huey Lewis, Cyndi Lauper, Kim Carnes, Bob Dylan and Ray Charles.

We Are The World spent four weeks at no.1 in the United States, where it went 4 x Platinum, denoting a shipment of eight million singles. It was the no.1 bestselling single of 1985 in the United States, and also hit no.1 in Australia, Belgium, France, Ireland, Italy, the Netherlands, New Zealand, Norway, South Africa, Sweden, Switzerland and the UK, no.2 in Austria and Germany, and no.3 in Canada.

The estimated global sales of *We Are The World* are 9-10 million.

We Are The World won four Grammy Awards, for Record of the Year, Song of the Year, Best Pop Vocal Performance by a Duo or Group and Best Music Video, Short Form. It also picked up an American Music Award, for Song of the Year.

By the end of 1985, the USA Foundation for Africa had raised around $40 million, to aid famine relief in Africa.

19 ~ Show Some Respect

USA: Capitol Records B-5461 (1985).
B-side: *Let's Pretend We're Married.*

20.04.85: 65-53-45-41-40-38-**37**-47-78-91

UK: Not Released.

Canada
17.06.85: **50**

New Zealand
28.04.85: 47-x-**41**

Show Some Respect was written by Terry Britten and Sue Shifrin, and was recorded by Tina for her *PRIVATE DANCER* album. Outside Europe, where *I Can't Stand The Rain* was preferred, it was the final single released from the album and was a modest success, charting at no.37 in the United States, no.41 in New Zealand and no.50 in Canada.

The B-side of *Show Some Respect* was a live cover of Prince's *Let's Pretend We're Married.*

20 ~ We Don't Need Another Hero (Thunderdome)

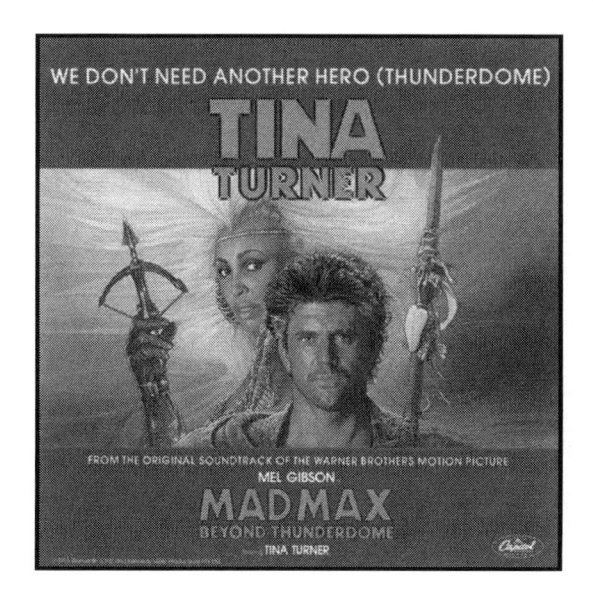

USA: Capitol Records B-5491 (1985).
  B-side: *We Don't Need Another Hero (Thunderdome) (Instrumental)*.

6.07.85: 52-41-32-26-20-14-10-6-4-3-**2**-4-12-22-43-61-92-99

UK: Capitol Records CL 364 (1985).
  B-side: *We Don't Need Another Hero (Thunderdome) (Instrumental)*.

20.07.85: 37-11-**3-3**-4-7-10-18-25-32-41-59-x-x-88

Australia
22.07.85: peaked at no.**1** (3), charted for 17 weeks

Austria
1.08.85: 19-5-3-**2**-4-9-15-23 (bi-weekly)

Belgium
20.07.85: 35-12-10-7-5-**3-3-3**-5-5-8-15-15-25-25-27

Canada
16.09.85: peaked at no.**1** (4), charted for 16 weeks

France
5.10.85: 14-9-6-**3-3**-4-5-5-9-9-7-15-24-19-25-36-45-41

A LONE WARRIOR SEARCHING FOR HIS DESTINY...A TRIBE OF LOST CHILDREN WAITING FOR A HERO...
IN A WORLD BATTLING TO SURVIVE, THEY FACE A WOMAN DETERMINED TO RULE.
HOLD OUT FOR MAD MAX
THIS IS HIS GREATEST ADVENTURE.
MEL GIBSON IS
MAD MAX
BEYOND THUNDERDOME
Starring TINA TURNER
KENNEDY MILLER Presents
MEL GIBSON TINA TURNER "MAD MAX BEYOND THUNDERDOME"
Music by MAURICE JARRE Director of Photography DEAN SEMLER A.C.S. Written by TERRY HAYES & GEORGE MILLER
Co-Produced by DOUG MITCHELL and TERRY HAYES Produced by GEORGE MILLER Directed by GEORGE MILLER and GEORGE OGILVIE
PG-13
READ THE WARNER PAPERBACK
DISTRIBUTED BY WARNER BROS.

Germany
22.07.85: 17-6-2-2-**1-1-1-1**-2-2-4-4-7-10-19-26-42-47-47-58-73

Ireland
28.07.85: 15-4-3-**2**-4-8-13-23

Italy
27.07.85: peaked at no.**2**, charted for 22 weeks

Netherlands
20.07.85: 21-16-8-8-8-**7**-11-13-14-20-25-26-33-35

New Zealand
18.08.85: 5-3-**2-2-2**-3-10-13-15-25-48

Norway
27.07.85: 8-7-4-4-3-3-4-**2-2**-4-3-3-5-7-x-9

South Africa
12.10.85: peaked at no.**9**, charted for 9 weeks

Spain
2.12.85: peaked at no.**1** (1), charted for 22 weeks

Sweden
9.08.85: **4-4**-6-7-14-17-14 (bi-weekly)

Switzerland
21.07.85: 15-3-**1-1-1-1-1-1**-2-3-3-5-5-8-9-30-25

Zimbabwe
19.10.85: peaked at no.**3**, charted for 12 weeks

We Don't Need Another Hero (Thunderdome) was written by Terry Britten and Graham Lyle for the 1985 film, *Mad Max Beyond Thunderdome*, which starred Tina alongside Mel Gibson. Tina's recording of the song featured a childrens choir from King's House School in Richmond, London.

We Don't Need Another Hero (Thunderdome) was released as the lead single from the accompanying soundtrack album, and gave Tina one of her biggest hits. The single went all the way to no.1 in Australia, Canada, Germany, Spain and Switzerland, and rose to no.2 in Austria, Ireland, Italy, New Zealand, Norway and the United States, no.3 in Belgium, France, the UK and Zimbabwe, no.4 in Sweden, no.7 in the Netherlands and no.9 in South Africa.

We Don't Need Another Hero (Thunderdome) was issued as a shaped 7" picture disc single in the UK.

We Don't Need Another Hero (Thunderdome) was nominated for a Golden Globe, for Best Original Song, but the award went to Lionel Richie's *Say You, Say Me,* from the film *White Nights.*

Tina picked up a Grammy nomination for *We Don't Need Another Hero (Thunderdome)*, for Best Pop Vocal Performance, Female, but she lost out to Whitney Houston and *Saving All My Love For You.*

21 ~ One Of The Living

USA: Capitol Records B-5518 (1985).
  B-side: *One Of The Living (Dub Version)*.

5.10.85: 52-40-37-31-27-21-17-**15-15**-26-39-64-73-78-83-90-91-92

UK: Capitol Records CL 376 (1985).
  B-side: *One Of The Living (Dub Version)*.

12.10.85: 61-**55**-77

Australia
21.10.85: peaked at no.**34**, charted for 8 weeks

Austria
15.11.85: 24-**12**-15-27-24 (bi-weekly)

Belgium
2.11.85: 20-**7**-**7**-14-27

Canada
23.12.85: peaked at no.**5**, charted for 14 weeks

Germany
21.10.85: 58-24-12-**6**-7-8-8-9-18-25-25-37-39-54-52-63

ONE OF THE LIVING
by HOLLY KNIGHT
Recorded by
TINA
TURNER
on CAPITOL RECORDS
Columbia Pictures Publications
Includes Professional
Fake Book Arrangement
4663OSMX / $2.95
THE MAKIKI PUBLISHING CO. LTD. ASCAP

Ireland
20.10.85: **15**-20

Netherlands
26.10.85: **13**-15-14-18-24-32-39

New Zealand
10.11.85: 43-43-30-35-**24**-25-25-25-25-25

Switzerland
3.11.85: 13-13-**9**-10-**9**-13-14-23-24

Zimbabwe
1.03.86: peaked at no.**17**, charted for 2 weeks

Tina recorded two new songs for the film *Mad Max Beyond Thunderdome*, and *One Of The Living* was the second of them. The song was composed by Holly Knight, and she also played keyboards and contributed backing vocals to the recording, which featured a saxophone solo by Tim Cappello.

One Of The Living couldn't match the success of *We Don't Need Another Hero (Thunderdome)*, but it did chart at no.5 in Canada, no.6 in Germany, no.7 in Belgium, no.9 in Switzerland, no.12 in Austria, no.13 in the Netherlands, no.15 in Ireland and the United States, no.17 in Zimbabwe, no.24 in New Zealand, no.34 in Australia and a lowly no.55 in the UK.

One Of The Living did triumph where *We Don't Need Another Hero (Thunderdome)* had fallen short, in that it won another Grammy Award for Tina, for Best Rock Vocal Performance, Female.

BRYAN/TINA
ADAMS TURNER
...TOGETHER!
IT'S ONLY LOVE
7" & 3-TRACK 12" SINGLE
FROM
THE BRYAN ADAMS ALBUM
"RECKLESS"
* TINA TURNER APPEARS
COURTESY OF CAPITOL RECORDS
A&M RECORDS
12" INCLUDES LIVE VERSION OF "IT'S ONLY LOVE"

22 ~ It's Only Love

USA: A&M Records AM-2791 (1985).
  B-side: *The Only One* (Bryan Adams).

23.11.85: 53-44-37-28-23-19-18-16-**15**-18-26-50-71-100

UK: A&M Records AM 285 (1985).
  B-side: *The Best Has Yet To Come* (Bryan Adams).

2.11.85: 54-36-31-**29**-32-55-x-x-x-78-77

Australia
10.02.86: peaked at no.**57**, charted for 8 weeks

Austria
15.02.86: **30** (bi-weekly)

Belgium
23.11.85: 40-**22**-30-34

Canada
16.12.85: peaked at no.**12**, charted for 13 weeks

Ireland
17.11.85: 20-**18**-23

Netherlands
23.11.85: 29-**21**-23-27-43

New Zealand
19.01.86: 39-**37**-45

Switzerland
8.12.85: 25-22-20-**16-16**-17-18-23-25

It's Only Love was written by Bryan Adams and Jim Vallance, and was recorded by Bryan Adams as a duet with Tina for his 1984 album, *RECKLESS*.

'When I heard *It's Only Love* the first time,' said Tina, 'I knew it was the song for me. Bryan came on as producer, the record was a hit, and we had such a good time performing it together that I invited him to come on tour with me.'

'Working with Tina was amazing,' said Bryan Adams. 'I used to go see her when I was in my late teens, early twenties, before she hit the big time. It was incredible to watch her. It was such a privilege to have sung with her, especially since I was only twenty-four at the time.'

Given it was the sixth and final single released from *RECKLESS*, *It's Only Love* did well to chart as highly as it did, peaking at no.12 in Canada, no.15 in the United States, no.16 in Switzerland, no.18 in Ireland, no.21 in the Netherlands, no.22 in Belgium, no.29 in the UK, no.30 in Austria, no.37 in New Zealand and no.57 in Australia.

The 12" single featured a live version of *It's Only Love*, which later was included on Tina's 1988 album, *LIVE IN EUROPE*.

Tina and Bryan Adams picked up a Grammy nomination for *It's Only Love*, for Best Rock Performance by a Duo or Group with Vocal, but the award went to Dire Straits for *Money For Nothing*.

23 ~ Typical Male

USA: Capitol Records B-5615 (1986).
  B-side: *Don't Turn Around.*

30.08.86: 49-39-27-19-13-9-5-**2-2-2**-8-20-33-52-74-100

UK: Capitol Records CL419 (1986).
  B-side: *Don't Turn Around.*

23.08.86: 43-34-**33**-36-39-48

Australia
22.09.86: peaked at no.**20**, charted for 17 weeks

Austria
1.10.86: 16-9-**6-6**-16-21-26 (bi-weekly)

Belgium
6.09.86: 37-21-21-21-20-18-27-**17**-18-25-39

Canada
27.10.86: peaked at no.**9**, charted for 13 weeks

France
18.10.86: 47-46-50-45-**31**-33-43-40-39

TYPICAL MALE

Lyrics and Music by GRAHAM LYLE & TERRY BRITTEN
Recorded by TINA TURNER on CAPITOL RECORDS

tina turner

ALMO PUBLICATIONS
GOOD SINGLE LIMITED &
MYAXE MUSIC LTD. (PRS)
ALMO MUSIC CORP

Germany
1.09.86: 50-9-6-**3**-4-5-4-6-9-13-18-24-38-49-56-61-74-74

Ireland
17.08.86: 26-14-**12**-20

Italy
13.09.86: peaked at no.**7**, charted for 16 weeks

Netherlands
30.08.86: 26-15-17-15-18-16-**14-14**-16-21-40

New Zealand
5.10.86: 28-17-**8**-10-10-13-17-16-19-22-21-36-36-36-36-42

Norway
30.08.86: 10-5-**2-2-2**-5-10-8-8

Spain
10.11.86: peaked at no.**1** (1), charted for 13 weeks

Sweden
27.08.86: 15-**6**-9-14-18 (bi-weekly)

Switzerland
31.08.86: 22-8-3-**2**-3-3-3-4-6-8-12-20-26-30

Typical Male was written by Terry Britten and Graham Lyle, and was recorded by Tina for her 1986 album, *BREAK EVERY RULE*. Phil Collins played drums on the recording.

Typical Male was released as the lead single from the album, and spent three weeks at no.2 in the United States, kept out of the top spot by Janet Jackson's *When I Think Of You* and Cyndi Lauper's *True Colors*.

Typical Male did hit no.1 in Spain, and charted at no.2 in Norway and Switzerland, no.3 in Germany, no.6 in Austria and Sweden, no.7 in Italy, no.8 in New Zealand, no.9 in Canada, no.12 in Ireland, no.14 in the Netherlands, no.17 in Belgium, no.20 in Australia, no.31 in France and no.33 in the UK.

Typical Male was issued as a 12" picture disc single in the UK.

The non-album B-side of *Typical Male*, *Don't Turn Around*, was composed by Albert Hammond and Diana Warren. Tina's original recording of the song isn't well known, but later covers by Luther Ingram, Aswad, Bonnie Tyler and Ace Of Base all did well.

In 1988, Aswad's reggae version of *Don't Turn Around* topped the chart in the UK and New Zealand, and was a Top 10 success in Belgium, Ireland, the Netherlands and Norway.

Ace Of Base's 1993 cover of *Don't Turn Around* went to no.1 in Canada, and was a Top 10 hit in a host of countries, including Austria, Finland, Germany, Ireland, the Netherlands, New Zealand, Sweden, the UK and the United States.

24 ~ Two People

USA: Capitol Records B-5644 (1986).
  B-side: *Havin' A Party*.

22.11.86: 72-54-45-41-38-31-31-**30-30**-48-68-99

UK: Capitol Records CL 430 (1986).
  B-side: *Havin' A Party*.

8.11.86: 52-**43**-51-70

Austria
1.01.97: **19**-29-25-25-26 (bi-weekly)

Belgium
29.11.86: **28**-36

Canada
8.12.86: peaked at no.**36**, charted for 6 weeks

Germany
3.11.86: 63-67-16-16-**10**-12-15-23-23-33-34-42-62-x-75

Ireland
9.11.86: 24-**23**

Italy
29.11.86: peaked at no.**18**, charted for 4 weeks

Netherlands
8.11.86: 42-24-**20**-22-27-50

New Zealand
18.01.87: **41**-46-**41**-x-45

Spain
16.02.87: peaked at no.**12**, charted for 6 weeks

Switzerland
23.11.86: 20-19-**10-10**-11-11-23-22

Two People was written by Terry Britten and Graham Lyle, and was recorded by Tina for her *BREAK EVERY RULE* album.

In North America, *Back Where You Started* was released as a promotional only single, as the follow-up to *Typical Male*, but it wasn't given a full commercial release. *Two People* was, and it charted at no.10 in Germany, no.12 in Spain, no.18 in Italy, no.19 in Austria, no.20 in the Netherlands, no.23 in Ireland, no.28 in Belgium, no.30 in the United States, no.36 in Canada, no.41 in New Zealand and no.43 in the UK.

Tina shot two different music videos to promote *Two People*, including a Hollywood version, which saw her playing several different characters.

A live version of *Two People* was included on Tina's 1988 album, *LIVE IN EUROPE*.

As with *Typical Male*, Tina released a non-album track on the B-side of *Two People*. This time, she chose to record a cover of *Havin' A Party*, which Sam Cooke wrote and originally recorded in 1962.

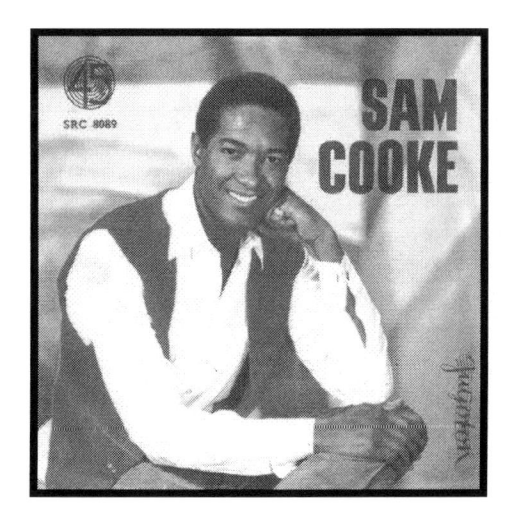

25 ~ What You Get Is What You See

USA: Capitol Records B-5668 (1987).
  B-side: *What You Get Is What You See (Live)*.

7.02.87: 74-56-50-41-32-25-22-15-**13**-15-29-49-58-83

UK: Capitol Records CL 439 (1987).
  B-side: *What You Get Is What You See (Live)*.

14.03.87: 43-37-**30**-32-38-54-72

Australia
23.02.87: peaked at no.**15**, charted for 28 weeks

Austria
1.04.87: 30-x-x-x-x-**23** (bi-weekly)

Belgium
6.06.87: **38**

Canada
13.04.87: peaked at no.**28**, charted for 8 weeks

Germany
23.02.87: 21-23-20-**17**-21-21-24-32-34-47-55-48-55-68

Ireland
15.03.87: 18-**16**-21

New Zealand
22.03.87: 45-44-44-x-**41-41**

What You Get Is What You See was written by Terry Britten and Graham Lyle, and was recorded by Tina ~ with Eric Clapton on guitar ~ for her *BREAK EVERY RULE* album. Tina is on record as saying it was her favourite song on the album.

Released as a single, *What You Get Is What You See* performed reasonably well, charting at no.13 in the United States, no.15 in Australia, no.16 in Ireland, no.17 in Germany, no.23 in Austria, no.28 in Canada, no.30 in the UK, no.38 in Belgium and no.41 in New Zealand.

As well as the live version featured on the B-side, live versions of *What You Get Is What You See* featured on Tina's *LIVE IN EUROPE* and *LIVE* albums, released in 1988 and 2009, respectively.

26 ~ Girls

USA & UK: Not Released.

Europe: Capitol Records 006 20 1619 7 (1986).
B-side: *Take Me To The River (Extended Version)*.

Netherlands
21.02.87: 46-28-23-**19**-28-37-52-68-81-81

After working with David Bowie on *Tonight*, Tina asked him if he would write a song for her.

'He said yes, but I doubted that he'd get around to doing it,' Tina wrote in her autobiography, *My Love Story*. 'Artists often said yes to me, and they meant well, but then they'd go off and get involved with their own lives and forget about it.'

David Bowie didn't forget: he called Tina a few months later, to tell her that he had a great song for her. 'It's called *Girls*,' he told her, 'and, if you don't take it, I'm going to do it.'

Tina knew, if David Bowie was happy to record it himself, it must be a good song and so it proved. She recorded *Girls* ~ with Phil Collins on drums ~ for her *BREAK EVERY RULE* album, and it was released as a single ahead of *What You Get Is What You See* in several European countries. However, although it rose to no.19 in the Netherlands, it failed to chart anywhere else.

The non-album B-side, *Take Me To The River*, was composed by Al Green and Mabon 'Teenie' Hodges, and was originally recorded by Al Green for his 1974 album, *AL GREEN EXPLORES YOUR MIND*.

27 ~ Break Every Rule

USA: Capitol Records B-44003 (1987).
  B-side: *Take Me To The River*.

9.05.87: 89-81-**74-74**-88

UK: Capitol Records CL 452 (1987).
  B-side: *Girls*.

6.06.87: 78-46-**43**-49

Australia
15.06.87: peaked at no.**60**, charted for 5 weeks

Austria
1.08.87: **21** (bi-weekly)

Germany
25.05.87: 51-49-**38**-57-49-57

Break Every Rule, which lent its name to Tina's 1986 album, was written by Rupert Hine and Jeannette Obstoj.
  With so many singles from the album having preceded it, *Break Every Rule* was only a modest hit, and only achieved Top 40 status in Austria and Germany, peaking at no.21 and no.38, respectively. It also achieved no.43 in the UK, and was a minor hit in Australia and the United States.

28 ~ Tearing Us Apart

USA: Warner Bros./Duck Records 7-28279 (1987).
  B-side: *Hold On* (Eric Clapton).

Tearing Us Apart wasn't a hit in the USA.

UK: Duck Records W 8299 (1987).
  B-side: *Hold On* (Eric Clapton).

20.06.87: 58-**56**-61

Belgium
8.08.87: **34-34**-35

Netherlands
1.08.87: 100-63-31-31-**30**-34-37-54-69

Tearing Us Apart was written by Eric Clapton and Greg Phillinganes, and was recorded by Eric Clapton as a duet with Tina for his 1986 album, *AUGUST* ~ the album was produced by Phil Collins.
  Tearing Us Apart was inspired by a group of Patti Boyd's friends 'the committee', whom Eric Clapton felt were responsible for coming between him and his girlfriend, and tearing them apart.
  Tearing Us Apart was released as the second single from *AUGUST*, after *Behind The Mask*, but like *Break Every Rule* it was only a minor hit, charting at no.30 in the

Netherlands, no.34 in Belgium and no.56 in the UK, but failing to chart at all in many countries.

Tina sang backing vocals on *Hold On*, the B-side of *Tearing Us Apart*, but she wasn't credited.

Tina and Eric Clapton performed *Tearing Us Apart* at The Prince's Trust All-Star Rock Concert, staged at London's Wembley Arena in 1986, to mark the trust's 10th anniversary. The charity concert also featured Ben E. King, Bryan Adams, Elton John, George Harrison, Midge Ure, Paul McCartney, Paul Young, Phil Collins and Rod Stewart.

Early the following year, a double album *THE ROYAL CONCERT* was released, which featured a live version of *Better Be Good To Me* by Tina, but omitted *Tearing Us Apart*.

A live version of *Tearing Us Apart* was included on Tina's 1988 album, *LIVE IN EUROPE*.

29 ~ Paradise Is Here

USA: Not Released.

UK: Capitol Records CL 459 (1987).
  B-side: *In The Midnight Hour (Live)*.

12.09.87: 79-**78**-95

Austria
15.10.87: 26-**25** (bi-weekly)

Germany
14.09.87: **31**-38-41-52-56-66

Ireland
24.05.87: 25-**21**

Paradise Is Here was composed by Paul Brady, who recorded the song for his 1987 album, *PRIMITIVE DANCE*.
  Tina recorded *Paradise Is Here* for her *BREAK EVERY RULE* album, and in Europe it was released as the follow-up to *Break Every Rule*. By now, however, everyone who was interested had already bought Tina's album, and *Paradise Is Here* was only a modest success. It charted at no.21 in Ireland, no.25 in Austria and no.31 in Germany, but stalled at a lowly no.78 in the UK.
  An edited live version of *Paradise Is Here* featured on Tina's 1988 album, *LIVE IN EUROPE*.

The B-side of *Paradise Is Here* was a live cover of Wilson Pickett's 1965 hit, *In The Midnight Hour*, which later featured on Tina's 1988 album, *LIVE IN EUROPE*.

Cher recorded a cover of *Paradise Is Here* for her 1995 album, *IT'S A MAN'S WORLD*. As a single, her version rose to no.11 on Billboard's Dance Club Songs in the United States, but it failed to enter any mainstream singles charts.

30 ~ Addicted To Love (Live)

USA: Not Released.

UK: Capitol Records CL 484 (1988).
  B-side: *Overnight Sensation*.

19.03.88: **71**-75

Belgium
16.04.88: **23**-28-28-33

Netherlands
26.03.88: 88-57-40-**28**-31-45-55-80

Addicted To Love was written by Robert Palmer, and he recorded the song himself for his 1985 album, *RIPTIDE*.
  As a single, promoted by an iconic music video featuring high fashion models dressed in black, *Addicted To Love* was a massive hit, going to no.1 in Australia and the United States, and achieving Top 5 status in a host of other countries, including Belgium, Canada, Ireland, New Zealand, South Africa and the UK.

Tina performed *Addicted To Love* regularly during her Break Every Rule Tour in 1986/87, and a live recording of the song was included on her 1988 album, *LIVE IN EUROPE*.

In some countries, *Addicted To Love* was chosen as the lead single from the album, ahead of *Nutbush City Limits*, and Tina's version charted at no.23 in Belgium and no.28 in the Netherlands, and was a minor no.71 hit in the UK.

A second live version of *Addicted To Love* by Tina featured on her 2009 album, *LIVE*.

31 ~ 634-5789 (Live)

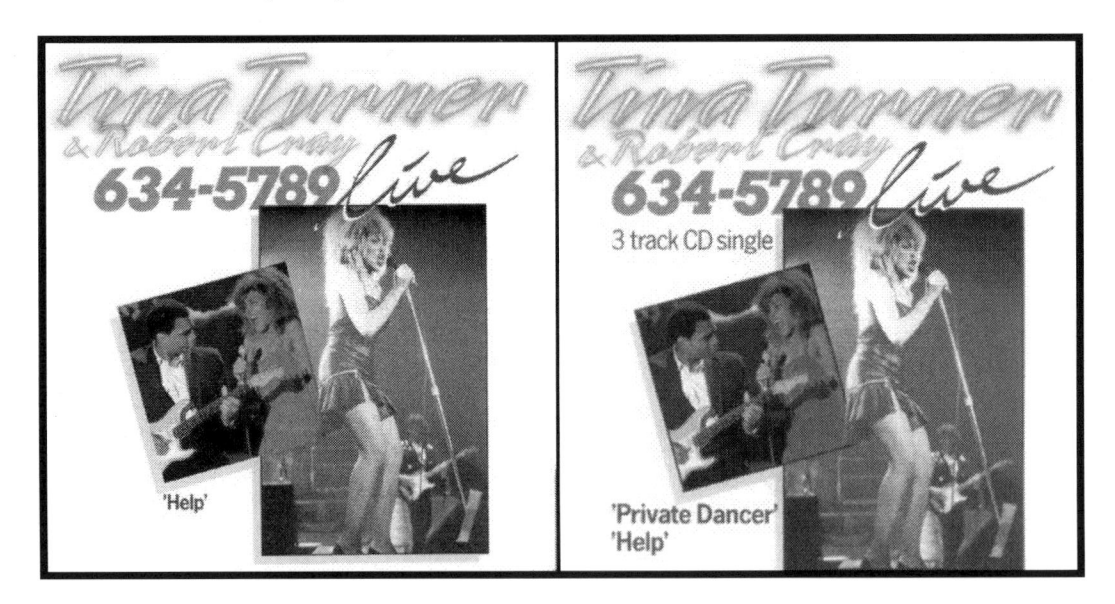

USA & UK: Not Released.

Netherlands: Capitol Records 006-203 279 7 (1989).

11.03.89: 75-34-25-17-**14**-17-29-41-73

Belgium
8.04.89: 36-32-37-**25**

634-5789 was written by Eddie Floyd and Steve Cropper, and was originally recorded by Wilson Pickett for his 1966 album, *THE EXCITING WILSON PICKETT*.

Wilson Pickett took *634-5789*, which was a reference to *Beechwood 4-5789* ~ a hit for the Marvelettes in 1962 ~ to no.1 on Billboard's Soul singles chart in the United States, and to no.13 on the Hot 100.

634-5789 was one of four classic soul hits Tina performed live with Robert Cray, during her 1986 TV special, *Break Every Rule*. The other three were Wilson Pickett's *In The Midnight Hour* and *Land Of 1000 Dances*, and Sam Cooke's *A Change Is Gonna Come*. All four live recordings were released on Tina's 1988 album, *LIVE IN EUROPE*.

634-5789 was only released as a single in a few countries, not including the UK or United States, and charted at no.14 in the Netherlands and no.25 in Belgium.

32 ~ The Best

USA: Capitol Records B-44442 (1989).
  B-side: *Undercover Agent For The Blues*.

2.09.89: 77-59-47-38-34-29-21-19-17-**15**-27-41-66-100

UK: Capitol Records CL 543 (1989).
  B-side: *Undercover Agent For The Blues*.

2.09.89: 31-16-10-**5-5**-7-12-19-24-32-42-68
1.05.10: 9-63

Australia
11.09.89: peaked at no.**5**, charted for 25 weeks
25.05.92: peaked at no.12, charted for 12 weeks (& Jimmy Barnes)
4.10.93: peaked at no.38, charted for 8 weeks

Austria
15.09.89: 6-3-**2**-3-5-5-10-14-20-29-27 (bi-weekly)

Belgium
9.09.89: 22-16-11-8-6-4-**2**-3-5-6-8-13-37

Canada
30.10.89: peaked at no.**2**, charted for 17 weeks

France
18.11.89: 46-40-42-29-27-28-**23**-28-30-28-43

Germany
28.08.89: 18-16-**4-4-4-4**-5-8-8-9-9-9-10-11-14-26-31-36-48-48-60-61-78-74-94-96

Ireland
3.09.89: 23-13-12-5-**4**-10

Italy
23.09.89: peaked at no.**2**, charted for 27 weeks

Netherlands
26.08.89: 32-15-10-9-9-**7-7**-9-14-23-27-41-58-80

New Zealand
1.10.89: 35-28-33-x-45-33-32
31.05.92: 13-22-**11**-17-17-21-28-35-44-x-49 (& Jimmy Barnes)

Norway
16.09.89: 8-9-**5**-7-7-10-10

Spain
16.10.89: **20**

Sweden
6.09.89: 13-12-**11**-14-19 (bi-weekly)

Switzerland
17.09.89: 8-6-5-**3**-4-5-5-9-8-8-10-12-10-14-16-16-16-21-23-24-30
1.03.09: 92

Zimbabwe
24.03.90: peaked at no.**8**, charted for 5 weeks

The Best (or *Simply The Best*, as it's commonly known) was written by Mike Chapman and Holly Knight, and the song was originally recorded by Bonnie Tyler for her 1988 album, *HIDE YOUR HEART* (titled *NOTES FROM AMERICA* in North America).

'*Simply The Best* is one of those rare gems,' said Holly Knight, 'that's a positive song, and it's not cheesy.'

As a single Bonnie Tyler's version of *The Best* charted at no.10 hit in Norway, no.20 in Spain and no.25 in Finland, but it struggled to no.95 in the UK, and failed to chart in most countries.

Tina recorded a cover of *The Best* for her 1989 album, *FOREIGN AFFAIR*. Released as the album's lead single, *The Best* was hugely successful, rising to no.2 in Austria, Belgium, Canada and Italy, no.3 in Switzerland, no.4 in Germany and Ireland, no.5 in Australia, Norway and the UK, no.7 in the Netherlands, no.8 in Zimbabwe, no.11 in Sweden, no.15 in the United States, no.20 in Spain, no.23 in France and no.28 in Australia.

Tina re-recorded *The Best* as a duet with Jimmy Barnes, an Australian rock singer, in 1992, to promote the New South Wales rugby league season in Australia. The duet was released as a single in Australasia only, where it charted at no.11 in New Zealand and no.12 in Australia.

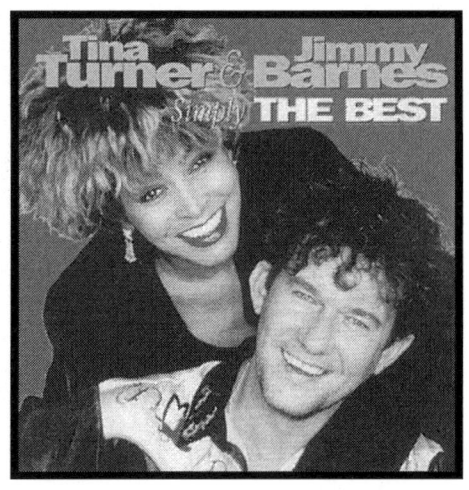

The duet version of *The Best* was featured on a 5-track limited edition bonus disc of Tina's 1991 compilation, *SIMPLY THE BEST*, in Australia.

33 ~ I Don't Wanna Lose You

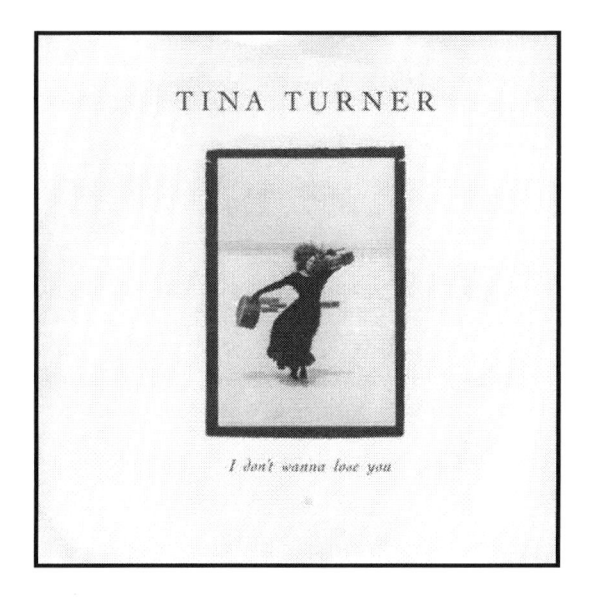

USA: Not Released.

UK: Capitol Records CL 553 (1989).
  B-side: *Not Enough Romance*.

18.11.89: 50-46-33-11-**8-8-8**-16-29-45-60

Australia
26.02.90: peaked at no.**74**, charted for 5 weeks

Austria
4.03.90: 29-27-25-**20-20**-22-23-28-26-27-28

Belgium
10.02.90: 31-29-22-16-**9-9**-11-11-22-24-38

Germany
26.02.90: 52-53-**38**-42-41-41-46-51-51-64-62-62-66-81-62-71-81-85-94

Ireland
19.11.89: 25-x-x-18-20-18-18-**16**-30

Netherlands
3.02.90: 83-56-44-34-30-26-**24**-27-39-65-81-100

Switzerland
18.03.90: **30**

I Don't Wanna Lose You was written by Albert Hammond and Graham Lyle, and was recorded by Tina for her *FOREIGN AFFAIR* album.

In Ireland and the UK, *I Don't Wanna Lose You* was released as the follow-up to *The Best*; in Australia and Europe, it was chosen as the third single from the album, but in North America it was passed over for single release.

I Don't Wanna Lose You was a Top 10 hit in the UK and Belgium, where it peaked at no.8 and no.9, respectively. Elsewhere, the single was only a modest hit, charting at no.16 in Ireland, no.20 in Austria, no.24 in the Netherlands, no.30 in Switzerland and no.38 in Germany.

34 ~ Steamy Windows

USA: Capitol Records B-44473 (1989).
  B-side: *The Best (Edit)*.

25.11.89: 83-69-61-53-48-48-**39**-42-63-75-97

UK: Capitol Records CL 560 (1990).
  B-side: *The Best (Single Muscle Mix)*.

17.02.90: 27-**13**-16-26-42-62

Australia
4.12.89: peaked at no.**37**, charted for 14 weeks

Austria
7.01.90: **18**-25-20-25-28-29-30

Belgium
25.11.89: 35-32-16-13-**5**-7-12-15-24-45

Canada
5.02.90: peaked at no.**25**, charted for 6 weeks

Germany
11.12.89: 58-51-**29-29**-31-34-33-35-58-58-66-66-71-73-85-94

Ireland
18.02.90: 10-**7**-13

Italy
2.12.89: peaked at no.**5**, charted for 10 weeks

Netherlands
18.11.89: 68-45-29-18-**16**-21-37-66-82-100

New Zealand
14.01.90: 41-49-**30**-37-x-40-47

Switzerland
3.12.89: **14**-17-16-18-18-17-23-27

Steamy Windows was composed by Tony Joe White, and was recorded by Tina for her *FOREIGN AFFAIR* album.

In most countries, *Steamy Windows* was the second single lifted from the album, after *The Best*. In Ireland and the UK, it was the album's third single, and was released as the follow-up to *I Don't Wanna Lose You*.

Charts and sales-wise, *Steamy Windows* performed better than *I Don't Wanna Lose You* had, rising to no.5 in Belgium and Italy, no.7 in Ireland, no.13 in the UK, no.14 in Switzerland, no.16 in the Netherlands, no.18 in Austria, no.25 in Canada, no.29 in Germany, no.30 in New Zealand, no.37 in Australia and no.39 in the United States.

35 ~ Foreign Affair

USA: Not Released.

Europe: Capitol Records 06 203859 7 (1990).
  B-side: *Private Dancer (Live in Europe)*.

Foreign Affair wasn't a hit in the UK.

Belgium
2.06.90: **49**

Germany
28.05.90: 77-51-**35**-39-45-46-53-51-53-67-63-68-72-72-72

Netherlands
2.06.90: 87-77-66-58-**55-55**-85

Like *Steamy Windows*, *Foreign Affair* was composed by Tony Joe White, and was recorded by Tina for her album with the same title.
  Foreign Affair was only issued as a single in a limited number of countries, and only achieved Top 40 status in one, Germany, where it rose to no.35. The single also charted at no.40 in Belgium and no.55 in the Netherlands, but it failed to chart in the other countries where it was released.

36 ~ Look Me In The Heart

USA: Capitol Records 4JM-44510 (Cassette Single, 1990).
  B-side: *Stronger Than The Wind*.

Look Me In The Heart wasn't a hit in the USA.

UK: Capitol Records CL 584 (1990).
  B-side: *Steel Claw (Live)*.

11.08.90: 41-34-**31**-33-42-59

France
17.03.90: **44-44**-45-50

Ireland
12.08.90: 28-**23**

Look Me In The Heart was written by Billy Steinberg and Tom Kelly, and was recorded by Tina for her *FOREIGN AFFAIR* album.
    As a single, *Look Me In The Heart* only enjoyed modest success, charting at no.23 in Ireland, no.31 in the UK and no.44 in France.
    Some formats of the single featured the *Tina Turner Montage Mix*, a nine minute megamix of songs from her *PRIVATE DANCER* and *BREAK EVERY RULE* albums.

37 ~ Be Tender With Me Baby

USA: Not Released.

UK: Capitol Records CL 593 (1990).
B-side: *Be Tender With Me Baby (Live)*.

13.10.90: 39-**28**-34-50

Ireland
14.10.90: **18**-21

Netherlands
13.10.90: 99-82-61-50-39-**35**-52-78

Be Tender With Me Baby was written by Albert Hammond and Holly Knight, and was recorded by Tina for her *FOREIGN AFFAIR* album.

Be Tender With Me Baby was only released as a single in Europe, where it achieved no.18 in Ireland, no.28 in the UK and no.35 in the Netherlands, but it failed to chart in most countries.

A seven minutes live version of *Be Tender With Me Baby* featured on the B-side, which was recorded at a concert at Woburn Abbey in Bedfordshire, England, during Tina's Foreign Affair Tour.

38 ~ It Takes Two

USA: Not Released.

UK: Warner Bros. Records ROD 1 (1990).
  B-side: *Hot Legs (Live)* (Rod Stewart).

24.11.90: 12-**5**-7-19-32-33-35-53

Australia
4.02.91: peaked at no.**14**, charted for 13 weeks

Austria
23.12.90: 19-19-**15**-20-**15**-16-20-21-22-27-29

Belgium
1.12.90: 32-18-8-7-**6**-8-8-8-10-18-22-47

Ireland
18.11.90: 12-**4**-**4**-11-25

Netherlands
24.11.90: 41-13-4-**3**-**3**-11-22-42-61-88

New Zealand
3.02.91: 24-26-**19**-26-25-25-25-34-21-21-21-37

Sweden
5.12.90: **11**-12-17 (bi-weekly)

Switzerland
16.12.90: 14-16-16-17-**10**-14-16-21-26

It Takes Two was written by Sylvia Moy and William 'Mickey' Stevenson, and was originally recorded in 1966 by Marvin Gaye & Kim Weston, who took the song to no.14 in the United States and no.16 in the UK.

Tina recorded a cover of *It Takes Two* with Rod Stewart, for his 1991 album, *VAGABOND HEART*. Later the same year, the duet featured on Tina's compilation album, *SIMPLY THE BEST*.

Tina and Rod Stewart's version of *It Takes Two*, which also featured in an advertising campaign for Pepsi, was released as the lead single from *VAGABOND HEART*. It charted at no.3 in the Netherlands, no.4 in Ireland, no.5 in the UK, no.6 in Belgium, no.10 in Switzerland, no.11 in Sweden, no.14 in Australia, no.15 in Austria and no.19 in New Zealand.

Surprisingly, *It Takes Two* wasn't released as a single in North America.

39 ~ Way Of The World

USA: Capitol Records (Cassette Single, 1991).
  B-side: *You Know Who (Is Doing You Know What*.

Way Of The World wasn't a hit in the USA.

UK: Capitol Records CL 637 (1991).
  B-side: *I Don't Wanna Lose You*.

23.11.91: 14-**13**-18-24-36-37-44

Austria
22.12.91: 27-28-28-**12**-22-19-23-24-16-16-21-23-17

Belgium
21.12.91: 39-23-40-26-19-**16**-17-19-27-48

France
15.02.92: 42-30-**25**-38-32-44-37-35-32-33-34-44-40-48

Germany
25.11.91: 90-51-36-**33**-34-34-**33**-45-43-46-51-51-53-53-58-61-73-74

Ireland
23.11.91: 18-**12**

WAY OF THE WORLD
TINA TURNER

WORDS & MUSIC BY G. LYLE / A. HAMMOND

RECORDED BY TINA TURNER ON CAPITOL RECORDS
PUBLISHED BY RONDOR MUSIC (LONDON) LIMITED / EMPIRE MUSIC LIMITED
£1.95

Netherlands
14.12.91: 71-58-44-30-25-20-**15**-24-42-62-95

Switzerland
26.01.92: 32-x-37-x-38-x-**29**

Way Of The World was written by Albert Hammond and Graham Lyle, and it was one of four new songs Tina recorded for her 1991 compilation album, *SIMPLY THE BEST*.

In most countries, *Nutbush City Limits (The 90s Version)* was the lead single from the album, with *Way Of The World* chosen as the follow-up.

Way Of The World sold reasonably well in most countries, and achieved no.12 in Austria and Ireland, no.13 in the UK, no.15 in the Netherlands, no.16 in Belgium, no.25 in France, no.29 in Switzerland and no.33 in Germany. However, *Way Of The World* failed to enter the Hot 100 in the United States.

40 ~ Love Thing

USA: Capitol Records C2-15786 (1991).
 Tracks: *Foreign Affair/Steamy Windows*.

Love Thing wasn't a hit in the USA.

UK: CDCL 644 (1991).
 Tracks: *I'm A Lady/It's Only Love (Live)/Private Dancer (Live)*.

15.02.92: **29**-38-57-75

Australia
16.03.92: peaked at no.**65**, charted for 4 weeks

Germany
2.03.92: 89-x-80-**67**-84-88-98

Netherlands
29.02.92: 91-78-52-44-**41-41**-49-73-93

Love Thing was written by Albert Hammond and Holly Knight, and was one of four new songs Tina recorded for her 1991 compilation, *SIMPLY THE BEST*.
 Released as the follow-up to *Way Of The World*, *Love Thing* only achieved Top 40 status in the UK, where it debuted at no.29 but rose no higher. The single also charted at no.41 in the Netherlands, and was a minor hit in Australia and Germany, but like *Way Of The World* it wasn't a hit in the United States.

41 ~ I Want You Near Me

USA: Not Released.

UK: Capitol Records CDCL 659 (1991).
Tracks: *Let's Stay Together/Tonight (Live)/Let's Dance (Live)*.

6.06.92: 39-**22**-44-60

Germany
25.05.92: 96-58-64-58-59-64-54-**53**-65-65-74-99

I Want You Near Me was written by Terry Britten and Graham Lyle, and it was one of four new songs Tina recorded for her 1991 compilation, *SIMPLY THE BEST*.

I Want You Near Me was the third of the new songs to be released as a single and, like *Love Thing*, it achieved Top 40 status in the UK but nowhere else. The single charted at no.22 in the UK, and was a minor no.53 hit in Germany, but it failed to chart anywhere else and was passed over for single release in North America.

42 ~ I Don't Wanna Fight

USA: Capitol Records 0 7777 12652 4 2 (Cassette Single, 1993).
B-side: *Tina's Wish*.

29.05.93: 83-66-66-58-41-37-25-17-15-12-10-**9**-11-13-16-15-19-20-27-30-33-38-41-45

UK: Parlophone 7243 880647 2 9 (1993).
Tracks: *Tina's Wish/I Don't Wanna Fight (Urban Mix)/(Holiday Inn Lounge Mix)*.

22.05.93: 15-**7**-9-14-15-22-35-54-66

Australia
28.06.93: peaked at no.**40**, charted for 22 weeks

Austria
11.07.93: 30-**29-29**-30

Belgium
29.05.93: 50-45-32-26-24-17-15-14-**8-8**-18-26-30

France
24.07.93: **43**

Germany
14.06.93: 52-51-39-**35**-38-42-36-47-54-55-54-57-57

113

ORIGINAL SHEET MUSIC EDITION

I DON'T WANNA FIGHT

Recorded by TINA TURNER on VIRGIN RECORDS
Words and Music by STEVE DUBERRY, LULU and BILLY LAWRIE

Ireland
30.05.93: **14-14**-19-26-28

Italy
10.07.93: peaked at no.**7**, charted for 7 weeks

Netherlands
29.05.93: 42-31-22-18-**14**-16-20-37-42

New Zealand
13.06.93: 12-**7**-15-9-**8**-9-**8**-15-25-26-x-44

Norway
29.05.93: **8**

Sweden
30.06.93: **39** (bi-weekly)

Switzerland
6.06.93: 25-25-15-**11**-16-**11**-**11**-12-13-14-**11**-28-25-24-26-28-25-25-37-34-39

Zimbabwe
28.08.93: peaked at no.**17**, charted for 2 weeks

I Don't Wanna Fight was written by Lulu, Billy Lawrie and Steve DuBerry, and was recorded by Tina for her autobiographical film and soundtrack album, *WHAT'S LOVE GOT TO DO WITH IT*, released in 1993. Lulu also recorded *I Don't Wanna Fight*, and her version featured as one of the tracks on her 1993 CD single, *How 'Bout Us*, released exclusively in the UK.

I Don't Wanna Fight was released as the lead single from *WHAT'S LOVE GOT TO DO WITH IT*, and it gave Tina her biggest hit since *The Best*. The single achieved no.7 in Italy, New Zealand and the UK, no.8 in Belgium and Norway, no.9 in the United States, no.11 in Switzerland, no.14 in Ireland and the Netherlands, no.17 in Zimbabwe, no.29 in Austria, no.35 in Germany, no.39 in Sweden, no.40 in Australia and no.43 in France.

Tina was nominated for a Grammy for *I Don't Wanna Fight*, for Best Pop Vocal Performance, Female, but Whitney Houston took the award for her mega-selling *I Will Always Love You*.

I Don't Wanna Fight picked up a second Grammy nomination, for Best Song Written Specifically for a Motion Picture or for Television, but the award went to *A Whole New World*, from *Aladdin*.

43 ~ Disco Inferno

USA: Not Released.

UK: Parlophone 7243 880858 2 3 (1993).
  Tracks: *I Don't Wanna Fight (Single Edit)/Disco Inferno (12" Version)/(12" Dub)*.

28.08.93: 14-**12**-15-29-43-58

Australia
25.10.93: peaked at no.**50**, charted for 7 weeks

Belgium
23.10.93: 49-46-28-21-21-18-12-12-12-**10**-14-14-23-32

Ireland
29.08.93: 27-**13**-16-20

Netherlands
13.11.93: 43-29-19-**17**-29-45

New Zealand
19.09.93: **25**-27-28-36-27-37

Disco Inferno was written by Leroy Green and Ron 'Have Mercy' Kersey, and it was originally recorded by the Trammps for their 1976 album with the same title. The following year, the song also featured on the hugely successful soundtrack album,

SATURDAY NIGHT FEVER. The Trammps took *Disco Inferno* to no.6 in Canada, no.11 in the United States, no.13 in New Zealand, no.16 in the UK and no.32 in Australia.

Tina recorded *Disco Inferno* for her 1993 soundtrack album, *WHAT'S LOVE GOT TO DO WITH IT*. Outside North America, it was released as the follow-up to *I Don't Wanna Fight*, and charted at no.10 in Belgium, no.12 in the UK, no.13 in Ireland, no.17 in the Netherlands, no.25 in New Zealand and no.50 in Australia.

Cyndi Lauper recorded a cover of *Disco Inferno* in 1999, which was nominated for a Grammy Award, for Best Dance Recording (Madonna took the award, for *Ray Of Light*).

44 ~ Why Must We Wait Until Tonight?

USA: Virgin Records V25H-38407 (1993).
Tracks: *Why Must We Wait Until Tonight? (7" Edit)/(Tony Dofat Remix)/(LP Version)/ (Tony Dofat Piano/Drums/Vocals Only)/Shake A Tail Feather/Why Must We Wait Until Tonight? (Acappella).*

23.10.93: **97**-100

UK: Parlophone 7243 881020 2 5 (1993).
Tracks: *The Best (Jimmy Barnes Version)/Shake A Tail Feather (Album Version)/Why Must We Wait Until Tonight? (Remix).*

30.10.93: **16**-17-36-54
1.01.94: 98

Belgium
12.03.94: **49**

Germany
8.11.93: 56-56-56-**55**-58-61-56-62-62-98-83

Ireland
7.11.93: **25**

Why Must We Wait Until Tonight? was composed by Bryan Adams and Robert John 'Mutt' Lange, and was recorded by Tina for her soundtrack album, *WHAT'S LOVE GOT TO DO WITH IT*.

Released as the second single from the album in North America, and as the follow-up to *Disco Inferno* in most other countries, *Why Must We Wait Until Tonight?* was a modest success. It charted at no.16 in the UK, no.25 in Ireland, no.49 in Belgium and no.55 in Germany, but it only managed a very disappointing no.97 on the Hot 100 in the United States.

45 ~ GoldenEye

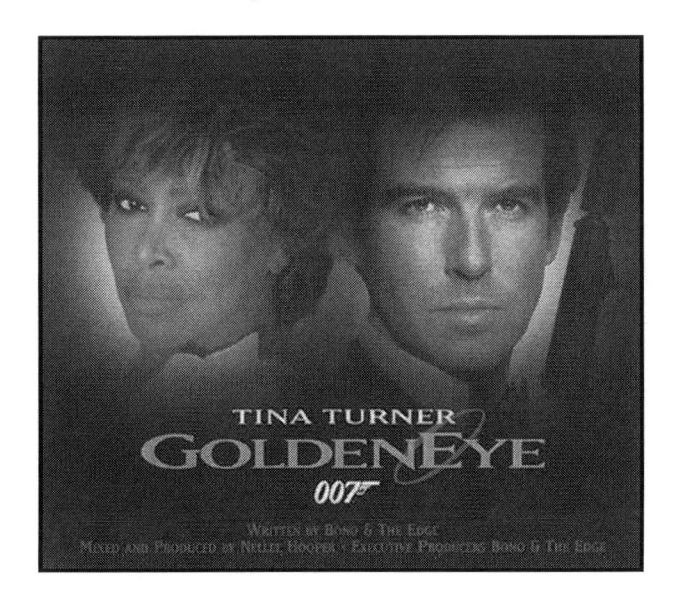

USA: Virgin Records 7243 838524 2 2 (1995).
Tracks: *GoldenEye (Edit)/(A/C Mix)/(Urban Mix)/(Club Edit)*.

GoldenEye failed to enter the Hot 100 in the United States, however, it did spend 10 weeks on the 'bubbling under' chart, peaking at no.2.

UK: Parlophone CDR007 (1995).
Tracks: *GoldenEye (Edit)/(Urban Mix)/(A/C Mix)/(Urban A/C Mix)/(Club Edit)*.

18.11.95: **10**-19-22-24-37-36-37-41-56-81

Australia
4.12.95: peaked at no.**72**, charted for 12 weeks

Austria
19.11.95: 22-17-11-6-8-8-8-9-**5**-7-7-9-10-16-19

Belgium
25.11.95: 32-26-27-22-16-19-14-10-**9**-14-13-17-22-23-26-27-26-34-39

Canada
12.02.96: peaked at no.**16**, charted for 9 weeks

Finland
4.11.95: **3**-**3**-**3**-4-10-9-5-7-5-5-9-9-20

007
GOLDENEYE
No limits. No fears. No substitutes.
ALBERT R. BROCCOLI PRESENTS PIERCE BROSNAN AS IAN FLEMING'S JAMES BOND 007 IN "GOLDENEYE" SEAN BEAN IZABELLA SCORUPCO
FAMKE JANSSEN AND JOE DON BAKER ERIC SERRA ANTHONY WAYE TERRY RAWLINGS PHIL MEHEUX PETER LAMONT TOM PEVSNER
MICHAEL FRANCE JEFFREY CAINE AND BRUCE FEIRSTEIN MICHAEL G. WILSON AND BARBARA BROCCOLI MARTIN CAMPBELL
BONO AND THE EDGE TINA TURNER
COMING SOON
UNITED ARTISTS

France
16.12.95: 39-11-8-5-5-5-5-**3**-5-6-6-12-16-24-35-44-46-42

Germany
20.11.95: 45-63-22-23-11-13-13-11-**8**-9-10-12-17-21-26-34-43-59-66-77-80

Ireland
16.11.95: 27-22-**15**-18-23

Italy
11.11.95: peaked at no.**5**, charted for 15 weeks

Netherlands
18.11.95: 34-21-**17-17**-18-22-22-26-26-30-42

Norway
2.12.95: 15-13-13-12-**9**-11-11-10-11-17

Sweden
17.11.95: 23-18-9-9-9-**6-6**-9-13-13-14-18-18-36-33-x-49-46

Switzerland
3.12.95: 8-9-4-4-4-4-**3**-4-6-9-10-12-15-19-26-28-27-27-41-36-43-x-34

Zimbabwe
22.01.96: peaked at no.**12**, charted for 2 weeks

GoldenEye was written by U2's Bono and The Edge, and was recorded by Tina as the theme song to the James Bond film with the same title.

Bono and The Edge had homes in Eze-sur-Mer, France, and invited Tina over for dinner one evening. Whilst she was there, they mentioned they were writing the theme song for the new James Bond film, and said they wanted her to sing it.

'I was thrilled … until I heard Bono's demo,' said Tina, 'which was strange little snippets of music that didn't add up to a real melody.'

Bono later admitted he realised the demo was really bad, but he and The Edge worked on it and eventually the song took shape.

'I think we recorded it in two or three takes,' said Tina. 'After that, I actually liked the way *GoldenEye* transformed my singing.'

GoldenEye was released in November 1995, a week or two before the first James Bond starring Pierce Brosnan as 007 premiered. The single was especially successful in Europe, where it achieved no.3 in Finland, France and Switzerland, no.5 in Austria and Italy, no.6 in Sweden, no.8 in Germany, no.9 in Belgium and Norway, no.10 in the UK, no15 in Ireland and no.17 in the Netherlands.

Outside Europe, *GoldenEye* was less popular, but it at charted at no.12 in Zimbabwe and no.16 in Canada, and was a minor hit in Australia. In the United States, the single spent ten weeks on the 'bubbling under' section of the Hot 100, rising to no.2, but it failed to enter the Hot 100.

GoldenEye was the lead song on the accompanying soundtrack album, but was Tina's only contribution to the soundtrack, with the rest of the album credited to Eric Serra.

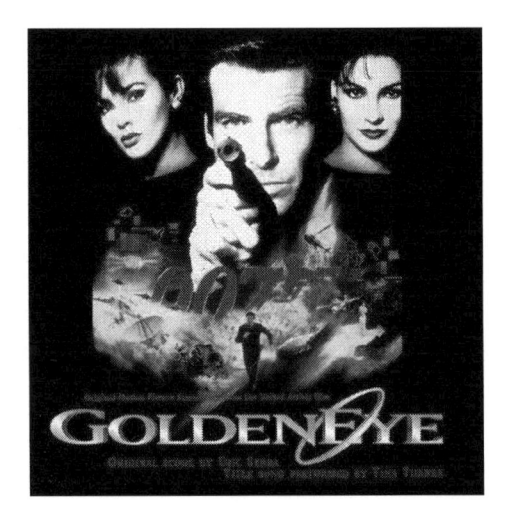

The following year, GoldenEye was released on Tina's *WILDEST DREAMS* album.

46 ~ Whatever You Want

USA: Not Released.

UK: Parlophone 7243 882743 2 6 (1996).
  Tracks: *GoldenEye (Single Edit)/Whatever You Want (Album Version)*.

23.03.96: **23**-24-46-54-67-75-88-x-x-85-x-93

Australia
20.05.96: **100**

Austria
17.03.96: 39-x-33-35-**27**-30-30-38-37

Belgium
23.03.96: **26**-28-31-39-28-36

Finland
2.03.96: 19-**9**-20

Germany
25.03.96: 58-73-**53**-55-56-56-59-64-62-66-71-85-98

Italy
9.03.96: peaked at no.**5**, charted for 9 weeks

125

Netherlands
16.03.96: 30-20-**18**-26-41

New Zealand
19.05.96: **16**-26-41

Sweden
8.03.96: **36**-43-48-48-x-42

Switzerland
10.03.96: 31-24-20-**18**-21-20-25-26-30-31-24-42-41-49-49

Whatever You Want was written by Arthur Baker, Taylor Dayne and Fred Zarr, and was recorded by Tina for her 1996 album, *WILDEST DREAMS*.

GoldenEye apart, *Whatever You Want* was released as the lead single from the album but, perhaps because of *GoldenEye*'s lack of success there, it wasn't issued in the United States.

Whatever You Want was moderately successful, charting at no.5 in Italy, no.9 in Finland, no.16 in New Zealand, no.18 in the Netherlands and Switzerland, no.23 in the UK, no.26 in Belgium, no.27 in Austria, no.36 in Sweden and no.53 in German.

Two CD singles were issued, with the second including Tina's cover of Massive Attack's *Unfinished Symphony*.

The song's co-writer, Taylor Dayne, recorded her own version of *Whatever You Want* for her 1998 album, *NAKED WITHOUT YOU*.

47 ~ On Silent Wings

USA: Not Released.

UK: Parlophone 7243 882905 2 4 (1996).
  Tracks: *Private Dancer/The Best/I Don't Wanna Lose You.*

8.06.96: **13**-25-35-49-57-66-86

Austria
4.08.96: 34-34-32-**30**-32-33-37-37

Belgium
8.06.96: 46-44-47-40-**36**-38-43

Germany
24.06.96: 69-69-56-**55**-56-56-56-58-61-66-69-85-88

Netherlands
1.06.96: 44-**37**-38

On Silent Wings was composed by James Ralston and Tony Joe White, and was recorded by Tina ~ with Sting on guest vocals ~ for her *WILDEST DREAMS* album.
  Released as the follow-up to *Whatever You Want*, *On Silent Wings* performed best in the UK, where it made its chart debut at no.13, but it rose no higher. The single also achieved no.30 in Austria, no.36 in Belgium, no.37 in the Netherlands and no.55 in Germany.

48 ~ Missing You

USA: Virgin Records 7243 838553 2 2 (1996).
Tracks: *Do Something/We Don't Need Another Hero (Thunderdome)*.

5.10.96: 95-95-95-90-**84-84**-93-96-98

UK: Parlophone 7243 883085 2 6 (1996).
Tracks: *The Difference Between Us/Whatever You Want (Todd Terry Mix)/Missing You (Alternative Mix)*.

27.07.96: **12**-23-38-59-66-83

Germany
9.09.96: 69-72-**66-66**-69-70-71-80-90

Missing You was written by John Waite, Charles Sandford and Mark Leonard, and was originally recorded by John Waite for his 1984 album, *NO BRAKES*.
   As the lead single from the album, John Waite saw the single go to no.1 in Canada and the United States. On the Hot 100, the single that *Missing You* replaced at the top of the chart was Tina's *What's Love Got To Do With It*.
   Missing You was also a Top 10 hit in Australia, Ireland and the UK, peaking at no.5, no.6 and no.9, respectively.

Tina recorded a cover of *Missing You* for her *WILDEST DREAMS* album. Released as the follow-up to *Whatever You Want*, Tina's version charted at no.12 in the UK, but it wasn't a Top 40 hit anywhere else.

In the United States, with *Whatever You Want* only having been released as a promotional CD and 12" single, *Missing You* was the first single from *WILDEST DREAMS* to be granted a full release, but it stalled at a lowly no.84 on the Hot 100.

49 ~ Something Beautiful Remains

USA: Not Released.

UK: Parlophone 7243 883339 2 4 (1996).
   Tracks: *Something Beautiful Remains ('Joe' Urban Remix Edit)/(Original Album Version)/('Joe' Urban Remix)*.

19.10.96: **27**-54-76-91

Something Beautiful Remains was written by Terry Britten and Graham Lyle, and was recorded by Tina for her *WILDEST DREAMS* album.
   Something Beautiful Remains was only released as a single in Europe and, like *Missing You*, it owes its Top 40 status to its performance in the UK, where it debuted at no. 27, before tumbling out of the Top 40 the following week. The single charted for four weeks, but it wasn't a hit anywhere else.

50 ~ In Your Wildest Dreams

USA: Virgin Records 7243 838438 2 4 (1996).
  Tracks: *In Your Wildest Dreams (Joe Remix Edit)/(Antonio Banderas Latin Mix)/ (Crossover Mix)*.

In Your Wildest Dreams failed to enter the Hot 100 in the USA, however, it did spend 15 weeks on the 'bubbling under' chart, peaking at no.1.

UK: Parlophone 7243 883551 2 4 (1996).
  Tracks: *In Your Wildest Dreams (Joe Urban Extended Mix)/(Antonio Slow Mix)*.

21.12.96: **32**-37-44-85

Australia
10.03.97: peaked at no.**68**, charted for 5 weeks

Austria
8.12.96: 27-16-7-7-4-**2**-5-5-8-10-10-10-17-20

Belgium
30.11.96: 39-27-**18**-19-22-19-**18**-22-32-33-30-35-46

Germany
25.11.96: 65-59-48-45-38-38-**32**-42-36-35-38-45-52-57

Netherlands
21.12.96: 87-83-78-**77**

New Zealand
23.02.97: 25-32-23-23-46-39-33-**22**-27-45

Norway
28.06.97: **15**

In Your Wildest Dreams was written by Mike Chapman and Holly Knight, and was recorded by Tina as a duet with Barry White, for her *WILDEST DREAMS* album. The original album version, as released in Europe, featured spoken vocals by the Spanish actor Antonio Banderas.

In Your Wildest Dreams was the final single lifted from *WILDEST DREAMS*, and it was promoted with a claymation video featuring Tina and Barry White, with cameo appearances by Antonio Banderas and Wallace & Gromit.

In Your Wildest Dreams returned Tina to the charts in several countries, peaking at no.2 in Austria, no.15 in Norway, no.18 in Belgium, no.22 in New Zealand, and no.32 in Germany and the UK. The single was also a minor hit in Australia and the Netherlands, and spent 15 weeks 'bubbling under' the Hot 100 in the United States, without ever entering the Hot 100.

51 ~ *Cose Della Vita* – Can't Stop Thinking About You

USA: DDD 74321 55187-2 (1997).
  Tracks: *Taxi Story* (Eros Ramazzotti).

Europe: DDD 74321 55305 2 (1997).
  Tracks: *Taxi Story* (Eros Ramazzotti)/*Un Grosso No* (Eros Ramazzotti).

Cose Della Vita – Can't Stop Thinking Of You wasn't a hit in the USA or UK.

Austria
25.01.98: 35-35-20-19-14-18-17-17-14-11-13-**10**-11-12-13-17-18

Belgium
24.01.98: 22-**21**-28-25-24-22-30-35-36-42-50

France
28.02.98: 18-10-10-11-**6**-10-13-13-13-15-22-22-25-28-30-46-37-60-64-61-70-90-92

Germany
2.02.98: 38-34-20-13-9-8-5-**4**-**4**-5-8-9-10-13-12-11-18-17-19-20-25-30-31-36-38-42-52-66

Netherlands
17.01.98: 65-17-12-7-6-5-**4**-7-6-6-11-15-16-21-29-30-39-32-33-51-62-70-73-78

Sweden
30.01.98: 43-39-**37**-44-x-56-58

Switzerland
1.02.98: 17-14-13-10-10-10-8-8-8-9-9-**7**-12-14-14-16-17-20-18-27-30-30-31-33-34-31-32-36

Cose Della Vita (which translates as 'Things In Life') was written by Eros Ramazzotti, Adelio Cogliati and Piero Cassano, and was originally recorded by Eros Ramazzotti ~ an Italian singer-songwriter ~ for his 1993 album, *TUTTE STORIE*. As a single, *Cose Della Vita* was a Top 5 hit in Belgium, Italy and Spain, and proved very popular in Latin America.

Eros Ramazzotti recorded a bilingual English/Italian version of *Cose Della Vita*, sub-titled *Can't Stop Thinking Of You*, as a duet with Tina for his 1997 greatest hits album, *EROS*. The English lyrics were penned by Tina and James Ralston.

Although it missed the charts in both the United States and the UK, *Cose Della Vita – Can't Stop Thinking Of You* proved very popular in continental Europe, where it charted at no.4 in Germany and the Netherlands, no.6 in France, no.7 in Switzerland, no.10 in Austria, no.21 in Belgium and no.37 in Sweden.

Tina included the duet on her 2004 compilation, *ALL THE BEST*, and on her compilation *THE PLATINUM COLLECTION*, released five years later.

Using Tina's English vocals, Eros Ramazzotti also recorded an English/Spanish version of *Cose Della Vita – Can't Stop Thinking Of You* ~ re-titled *Cosas De La Vida – Can't Stop Thinking Of You* ~ in 1997.

52 ~ When The Heartache Is Over

USA: Virgin Records 72438 38691 7 6 (7" Single, 1999).
  B-side: *On Silent Wings*.

When The Heartache Is Over wasn't a hit in the USA.

UK: Parlophone 7243 887855 2 5 (1999).
  Tracks: *I Can't Stand The Rain (Live in Amsterdam)/On Silent Wings (Live in Amsterdam)*.

30.10.99: **10**-19-23-36-45-55-62

Austria
31.10.99: **22**-29-26-30-**22**-31-37

Belgium
23.10.99: 45-19-**17**-23-24-26-30-34-35-40-43-43

Finland
9.10.99: **3**-3-5-4-7-8-16

France
27.11.99: 63-**49**-52-53-54-63-63-74-84-78-88

Germany
1.11.99: **23**-39-33-46-32-44-36-45-44-44-52-65

Italy
23.10.99: peaked at no.**19**, charted for 7 weeks

Netherlands
23.10.99: 43-**23**-25-33-33-34-39-41-47-53-62-72-91

Spain
1.11.99: 19-12-**11**-14-14

Sweden
28.10.99: 18-25-27-**16**-19-32-34-37-47-52

Switzerland
31.10.99: **17**-18-22-31-30-26-26-27-35-35-45-50-54-51-56-55-63-58-91

When The Heartache Is Over was composed by Graham Stack and John Reid, and was recorded by Tina for her 1999 album, *TWENTY FOUR SEVEN*.

Released as the lead single from the album, *When The Heartache Is Over* charted at no.3 in Finland, no.10 in the UK, no.11 in Spain, no.16 in Sweden, no.17 in Belgium and Switzerland, no.19 in Italy, no.22 in Austria, no.23 in Germany and the Netherlands, and no.49 in France.

In the United States, *When The Heartache Is Over* failed to enter the Hot 100, but it did rise to no.3 on Billboard's Hot Dance Club Songs chart.

53 ~ Whatever You Need

USA: Not Released.

UK: Parlophone 7243 888186 2 9 (2000).
   Tracks: *River Deep Mountain High (Recorded Live in London '99)*.

12.02.00: **27**-41-64-93-97-x-x-x-89

Finland
1.01.00: **11**-19-13

Germany
5.06.00: 90-90-94-89-**82**-83-92-83-91

Netherlands
29.01.00: 84-**72-72**-79-89-98

Whatever You Need was written by Harriet Roberts and Russell Courtney, and was recorded by Tina for her *TWENTY FOUR SEVEN* album.
   Released as the second single from the album, *Whatever You Need* couldn't match the success of *When The Heartache Is Over*, but it did achieve no.11 in Finland and no.27 in the UK, and it was a minor hit in Germany and the Netherlands.
   The various formats of the single included live versions of *River Deep – Mountain High*, *Steamy Windows*, *The Best* and *What's Love Got To Do With It*, all recorded at Tina's 60th birthday celebration in London in November 1999.

54 ~ Open Arms

USA: Not Released.

UK: Parlophone 7243 867657 2 7 (2004).
   Tracks: *The Best (Edit)*.

6.11.04: **25**-37-53-x-x-99-93

Austria
7.11.04: **31**-38-41-38-44-57-60-63-53-65-64

Germany
8.11.04: **33**-54-51-46-55-59-70-68-62

Italy
20.11.04: peaked at no.**22**, charted for 13 weeks

Netherlands
30.10.04: 73-72-**54**-71-79-79-78-80-91-95

Switzerland
7.11.04: **32**-45-80-83-87-70-x-93

Open Arms was written by Ben Barson, Colette van Sertima and Martin Brammer, and was one of three new songs Tina recorded for her 2004 compilation album, *ALL THE BEST*. The recording featured backing vocal by Estelle and KT Tunstall.

Released as the lead single from *ALL THE BEST*, *Open Arms* gave Tina a modest hit, charting at no.22 in Italy, no.25 in the UK, no.31 in Austria, no.32 in Switzerland, no38 in Germany and no.54 in the Netherlands.

Open Arms failed to enter the Hot 100 in the United States, but it did climb to no.15 on Billboard's Adult Contemporary chart.

55 ~ Let's Dance (Live)

No physical release.

Let's Dance (Live) wasn't a hit in the USA or UK.

France
16.01.16: **31**-70

Tina and David Bowie performed *Let's Dance* ~ actually two different songs ~ together at the National Exhibition Centre in Birmingham, England, on 23rd March 1985, on the same evening they performed *Tonight* together. Both live recordings were released on Tina's 1988 album, *LIVE IN EUROPE*.

Tina and David Bowie kicked off *Let's Dance* with a song composed by Jim Lee and recorded by Chris Montez in 1962. He took the song to no.1 in Belgium, no.2 in Norway and the UK, no.3 in the Netherlands and no.4 in the United States.

Tina and David Bowie followed Chris Montez's hit with David Bowie's own *Let's Dance*, which he wrote and recorded for his 1983 album with the same title. *Let's Dance* gave David Bowie one of the biggest hits of his career, hitting no.1 in Austria, Belgium, Canada, Finland, Ireland, the Netherlands, New Zealand, Norway, Spain, Sweden, Switzerland, the United States and the UK.

Five singles were released from Tina's *LIVE IN EUROPE* album in various countries, but *Let's Dance* wasn't one of them. However, in early 2016 it did enter the singles chart in France for two weeks, peaking at its debut position, no.31.

Let's Dance is the most recent track by Tina to achieve Top 40 status.

THE ALMOST TOP 40 SINGLES

Five of Tina's singles, four with Ike and one duet, have made the Top 50 in one or more countries, but failed to enter the Top 40 in any.

Tra La La La La

This was the second single released from Ike & Tina's 1963 album, *DYNAMITE!*, in North America. It rose to no.50 on the Hot 100 singles chart in the United States during a seven week chart run, but it wasn't a hit anywhere else.

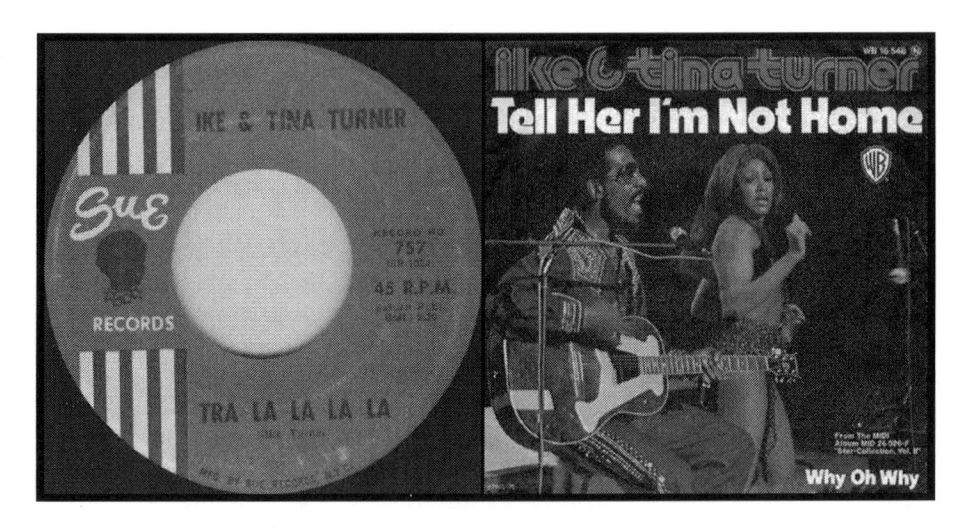

Tell Her I'm Not Home

Originally recorded by Chuck Jackson in 1963, Ike & Tina's cover of *Tell Her I'm Not Home* was a non-album recording that was released as a single in 1965 in North America, and the following year in Europe. The single failed to chart in the United States, but it did spend a solitary week at no.48 in the UK.

Sweet Rhode Island Red

Tina composed this song herself, and it was the title track of her and Ike's 1974 album. Released as the follow-up to *Nutbush City Limits*, *Sweet Rhode Island Red* wasn't a hit in the United States, but it did spend one week at no.43 on the chart in Germany. The single was a 'chart breaker' in the UK, but narrowly failed to enter the Top 50, and it wasn't a hit anywhere else.

Shame, Shame, Shame

This is a cover of a 1974 hit for Shirley & Company, and was one of several Ike & Tina recordings featured on Ike's 1980 solo album, *THE EDGE*. Released as a single in Europe in 1982, *Shame, Shame, Shame* entered the chart in the Netherlands at no.47, but it dropped out of the chart again the following week, and wasn't a hit anywhere else.

Teach Me Again

Tina recorded *Teach Me Again* as a duet with the Italian singer Elisa (Toffoli), for the soundtrack to the 2005 film, *All The Invisible Children*. Released as a single in Europe the following year, *Teach Me Again* charted at no.41 in Switzerland, no.43 in Germany and no.65 in Austria.

TINA'S TOP 40 SINGLES

In this Top 40, each of Tina's singles has been scored according to the following points system.

Points are given according to the peak position reached on the albums chart in each of the countries featured in this book:

    No.1:   100 points for the first week at no.1, plus 10 points for each additional week at no.1.

    No.2:   90 points for the first week at no.2, plus 5 points for each additional week at no.2.

    No.3:   85 points.
    No.4-6:   80 points.
    No.7-10:   75 points.
    No.11-15:   70 points.
    No.16-20:   65 points.
    No.21-30:   60 points.
    No.31-40:   50 points.
    No.41-50:   40 points.
    No.51-60:   30 points.
    No.61-70:   20 points.
    No.71-80:   10 points.
    No.81-100:   5 points.

Total weeks charted in each country are added, to give the final points score.

Reissues, remixes, alternate versions, live versions and re-entries of the same song are all counted together.

Rank/Single/Points

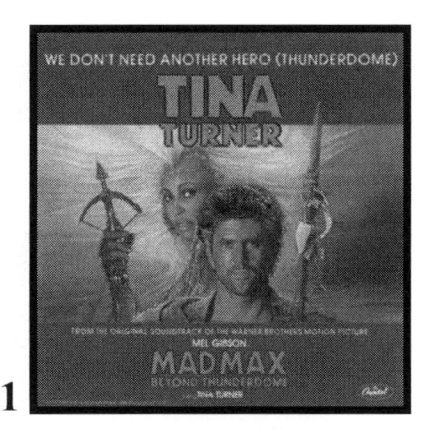

1 *We Don't Need Another Hero (Thunderdome) – 2038 points*

2 *What's Love Got To Do With It – 1729 points*

3 *The Best – 1608 points*

4 *Typical Male – 1428 points*

Rank/Single/Points

5 *Nutbush City Limits* – 1378 points

6 *GoldenEye* – 1274 points

7 *I Don't Wanna Fight* – 1119 points

8 *One Of The Living* – 899 points

9 *Steamy Windows* – 892 points

Rank/Single/Points

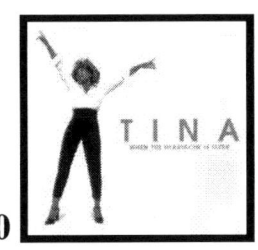

10. *When The Heartache Is Over* – 820 points

11. *Two People* – 803 points
12. *Let's Stay Together* – 792 points
13. *It Takes Two* – 761 points
14. *Private Dancer* – 759 points
15. *Whatever You Want* – 692 points

16. *It's Only Love* – 659 points
17. *Cose Della Vita* – 637 points
18. *What You Get Is What You See* – 624 points
19. *Way Of The World* – 594 points
20. *Better Be Good To Me* – 592 points

21. *I Don't Wanna Lose You* – 537 points
22. *Tonight* – 498 points
23. *In Your Wildest Dreams* – 480 points
24. *Disco Inferno* – 423 points
25. *Proud Mary* – 419 points

26. *I Can't Stand The Rain* – 361 points
27. *Open Arms* – 355 points
28. *On Silent Wings* – 298 points
29. *River Deep – Mountain High* – 276 points
30. *Why Must We Wait Until Tonight?* – 220 points

31. *Break Every Rule* – 212 points
32. *Help* – 199 points
33. *Paradise Is Here* – 195 points
34. *Be Tender With Me Baby* – 189 points
35. *Whatever You Need* – 169 points

Rank/Single/Points

36. *Baby – Get It On* – 163 points
36. *Love Thing* – 163 points
38. *Look Me In The Heart* – 162 points
39. *Tearing Us Apart* – 155 points
40. *Sexy Ida* – 151 points

We Don't Need Another Hero (Thunderdome), from her 1985 film *Mad Max Beyond Thunderdome*, emerges as Tina's most successful single, ahead of *What's Love Got To Do With It* and *The Best*, with *Typical Male* and *Nutbush City Limits* rounding off the Top 5.

The Top 40 includes five singles that were credited to Ike & Tina Turner, while her most successful post-Ike duet is *It Takes Two* with Rod Stewart, which is at no.13 on the list.

Tina's most recent Top 40 success to make this Top 40 is her 2004 hit, *Open Arms*.

SINGLES TRIVIA

To date, Tina has achieved fifty-five Top 40 singles in one or more of the countries featured in this book.

There follows a country-by-country look at Tina's most successful hits, starting with the country of her birth.

Note: in the past, there was often one or more weeks over Christmas and New Year when no new chart was published in some countries. In such cases, the previous week's chart has been used to complete chart runs. Similarly, where a bi-weekly or monthly chart was in place, for chart runs these are counted as two and four weeks, respectively.

TINA IN THE USA

Tina has achieved 38 hit singles in the United States, which spent 407 weeks on the Hot 100.

No.1 Singles

1984   *What's Love Got To Do With It*

What's Love Got To Do With It topped the chart for three weeks.

Singles with the most Hot 100 weeks

28 weeks	*What's Love Got To Do With It*
24 weeks	*I Don't Wanna Fight*
21 weeks	*Better Be Good To Me*
18 weeks	*I Want To Take You Higher*
18 weeks	*Private Dancer*
18 weeks	*We Don't Need Another Hero (Thunderdome)*
18 weeks	*One Of The Living*
16 weeks	*Typical Male*
15 weeks	*It's Gonna Work Out Fine*
15 weeks	*Nutbush City Limits*
15 weeks	*Let's Stay Together*

RIAA (Recording Industry Association of America) Awards

The RIAA began certifying Gold singles in 1958 and Platinum singles in 1976. From 1958 to 1988: Gold = 1 million, Platinum = 2 million. From 1988 onwards: Gold = 500,000, Platinum = 1 million. Awards are based on shipments, not sales (unless the award is for digital sales).

Gold	*Proud Mary* (May 1971)	= 1 million
Gold	*What's Love Got To Do With It* (August 1984)	= 1 million

TINA IN AUSTRALIA

Tina has achieved 22 hit singles in Australia, which spent 257 weeks on the chart.

No.1 Singles

1984	*What's Love Got To Do With It*
1985	*We Don't Need Another Hero (Thunderdome)*

We Don't Need Another Hero (Thunderdome) topped the chart for three weeks, and *What's Love Got To Do With It* for one week.

Singles with the most weeks

67 weeks	*Nutbush City Limits*
45 weeks	*The Best*
28 weeks	*What You Get Is What You See*
22 weeks	*What's Love Got To Do With It*
22 weeks	*I Don't Wanna Fight*
18 weeks	*Let's Stay Together*
18 weeks	*Better Be Good To Me*
17 weeks	*We Don't Need Another Hero (Thunderdome)*
17 weeks	*Typical Male*
15 weeks	*Private Dancer*

TINA IN AUSTRIA

Tina has achieved 25 hit singles in Austria, which spent 259 weeks on the chart.

No.1 Singles

1974	*Nutbush City Limits*

Nutbush City Limits topped the chart for one month.

Singles with the most weeks

20 weeks	*Nutbush City Limits*
18 weeks	*The Best*
17 weeks	*Cose Della Vita – Can't Stop Thinking Of You*
16 weeks	*We Don't Need Another Hero (Thunderdome)*
15 weeks	*GoldenEye*
14 weeks	*Typical Male*
14 weeks	*In Your Wildest Dreams*
13 weeks	*Way Of The World*
12 weeks	*What's Love Got To Do With It*
12 weeks	*I Can't Stand The Rain*
12 weeks	*Open Arms*

TINA IN BELGIUM (Flanders)

Tina has achieved 33 hit singles in Belgium (Flanders), which spent 271 weeks on the chart.

Her most successful single is *The Best*, which peaked at no.2.

Singles with the most weeks

19 weeks	*GoldenEye*
16 weeks	*We Don't Need Another Hero (Thunderdome)*
14 weeks	*Tonight (Live)*
14 weeks	*Disco Inferno*
13 weeks	*Nutbush City Limits*
13 weeks	*The Best*
13 weeks	*I Don't Wanna Fight*
13 weeks	*In Your Wildest Dreams*
12 weeks	*It Takes Two*
12 weeks	*When The Heartache Is Over*

TINA IN CANADA

Tina has achieved 13 hit singles in Canada, which have spent 135 weeks on the chart.

No.1 Singles

1984   *What's Love Got To Do With It*
1985   *We Don't Need Another Hero (Thunderdome)*

We Don't Need Another Hero (Thunderdome) topped the chart for four weeks, and *What's Love Got To Do With It* for one week.

Singles with the most weeks

18 weeks   *What's Love Got To Do With It*
17 weeks   *The Best*
16 weeks   *We Don't Need Another Hero (Thunderdome)*
14 weeks   *One Of The Living*
13 weeks   *It's Only Love*
13 weeks   *Typical Male*
11 weeks   *Better Be Good To Me*
 9 weeks   *GoldenEye*
 8 weeks   *What You Get Is What You See*

TINA IN FINLAND

Tina has achieved four hit singles in Finland, which spent 26 weeks on the chart.

Her most successful singles are *GoldenEye* and *When The Heartache Is Over*, which both peaked at no.3.

Singles with the most weeks

13 weeks   *GoldenEye*
 7 weeks   *When The Heartache Is Over*
 3 weeks   *Whatever You Want*
 3 weeks   *Whatever You Need*

TINA IN FRANCE

Tina has achieved 11 hit singles in France, which spent 127 weeks on the chart.

Her most successful singles are *We Don't Need Another Hero (Thunderdome)* and *GoldenEye,* which both peaked at no.3.

Singles with the most weeks

23 weeks	*Cose Della Vita – Can't Stop Thinking Of You*
18 weeks	*We Don't Need Another Hero (Thunderdome)*
18 weeks	*GoldenEye*
16 weeks	*What's Love Got To Do With It*
14 weeks	*Way Of The World*
11 weeks	*The Best*
11 weeks	*When The Heartache Is Over*
9 weeks	*Typical Male*

TINA IN GERMANY

Tina has achieved 36 hit singles in Germany, which spent 516 weeks on the chart.

No.1 Singles

1985   *We Don't Need another Hero (Thunderdome)*

We Don't Need another Hero (Thunderdome) topped the chart for four weeks.

Singles with the most weeks

44 weeks	*Nutbush City Limits*
28 weeks	*Cose Della Vita – Can't Stop Thinking Of You*
25 weeks	*The Best*
24 weeks	*What's Love Got To Do With It*
21 weeks	*We Don't Need Another Hero (Thunderdome)*
21 weeks	*GoldenEye*
19 weeks	*I Don't Wanna Lose You*
18 weeks	*Typical Male*
18 weeks	*Way Of The World*
16 weeks	*One Of The Living*
16 weeks	*Steamy Windows*

TINA IN IRELAND

Tina has achieved 24 hit singles in Ireland, which spent 97 weeks on the chart.

Her most successful single is *We Don't Need Another Hero (Thunderdome)*, which peaked at no.2.

Singles with the most weeks

9 weeks	*What's Love Got To Do With It*
8 weeks	*We Don't Need Another Hero (Thunderdome)*
7 weeks	*Let's Stay Together*
7 weeks	*I Don't Wanna Lose You*
6 weeks	*Private Dancer*
6 weeks	*The Best*

TINA IN ITALY

Tina has achieved 13 hit singles in Italy, which spent 163 weeks on the chart.

Her most successful singles are *We Don't Need Another Hero (Thunderdome)* and *The Best*, which both peaked at no.2.

Singles with the most weeks

27 weeks	*The Best*
27 weeks	*Nutbush City Limits*
22 weeks	*We Don't Need Another Hero (Thunderdome)*
16 weeks	*Typical Male*
15 weeks	*GoldenEye*
13 weeks	*Open Arms*
10 weeks	*Steamy Windows*
9 weeks	*Whatever You Want*

TINA IN JAPAN

Surprisingly none of Tina's singles, with Ike or solo, have charted in Japan.

TINA IN THE NETHERLANDS

Tina has achieved 38 hit singles in the Netherlands, which spent 369 weeks on the chart.

No.1 Singles

1989   *Tonight (Live)*

Tonight (Live) topped the chart for two weeks.

Singles with the most weeks

24 weeks	*Cose Della Vita – Can't Stop Thinking Of You*
20 weeks	*Nutbush City Limits*
19 weeks	*Tonight*
16 weeks	*Proud Mary*
14 weeks	*We Don't Need Another Hero (Thunderdome)*
14 weeks	*The Best*
13 weeks	*When The Heartache Is Over*
12 weeks	*Private Dancer*
12 weeks	*I Don't Wanna Lose You*
11 weeks	*Baby, Baby, Get It On*
11 weeks	*What's Love Got To Do With It*
11 weeks	*Typical Male*
11 weeks	*Way Of The World*
11 weeks	*GoldenEye*

TINA IN NEW ZEALAND

Tina has achieved 20 hits singles in New Zealand, which spent 187 weeks on the chart.

Her most successful single is *We Don't Need Another Hero (Thunderdome)*, which peaked at no.2.

Singles with the most weeks

19 weeks	*What's Love Got To Do With It*
17 weeks	*Let's Stay Together*
16 weeks	*Typical Male*
16 weeks	*The Best*
12 weeks	*It Takes Two*
11 weeks	*Tonight*
11 weeks	*We Don't Need Another Hero (Thunderdome)*
11 weeks	*I Don't Wanna Fight*
10 weeks	*Private Dancer*
10 weeks	*One Of The Living*
10 weeks	*In Your Wildest Dreams*

TINA IN NORWAY

Tina has achieved eight hit singles in Norway, which spent 50 weeks on the chart.

Her most successful singles are *We Don't Need Another Hero (Thunderdome)* and *Typical Male*, which both peaked at no.2.

Singles with the most weeks

15 weeks	*We Don't Need Another Hero (Thunderdome)*
10 weeks	*GoldenEye*
9 weeks	*Typical Male*
7 weeks	*The Best*
6 weeks	*Ball Of Confusion*

TINA IN SOUTH AFRICA

Tina has achieved two hit singles in South Africa, which spent 28 weeks on the chart.

Her most successful singles are *What's Love Got To Do With It*, which peaked at no.2.

Singles with the most weeks

19 weeks	*What's Love Got To Do With It*
9 weeks	*We Don't Need Another Hero (Thunderdome)*

TINA IN SPAIN

Tina has achieved 11 hit singles in Spain, which spent 98 weeks on the chart.

No.1 Singles

1985	*We Don't Need Another Hero (Thunderdome)*
1986	*Typical Male*

Both singles topped the chart for one week.

Singles with the most weeks

22 weeks	*We Don't Need Another Hero (Thunderdome)*
21 weeks	*Private Dancer*
13 weeks	*Typical Male*
10 weeks	*Nutbush City Limits*
9 weeks	*What's Love Got To Do With It*
7 weeks	*River Deep – Mountain High*

TINA IN SWEDEN

Tina has achieved 10 hits in Sweden, which spent 92 weeks on the chart.

Her most successful singles are *What's Love Got To Do With It* and *We Don't Need Another Hero (Thunderdome)*, which both peaked at no.4.

Singles with the most weeks

17 weeks	*GoldenEye*
14 weeks	*We Don't Need Another Hero (Thunderdome)*
12 weeks	*What's Love Got To Do With It*
10 weeks	*Typical Male*
10 weeks	*The Best*
10 weeks	*When The Heartache Is Over*

TINA IN SWITZERLAND

Tina has achieved 19 hit singles in Switzerland, which spent 279 weeks on the chart.

No.1 Singles

1985   *We Don't Need Another Hero (Thunderdome)*

We Don't Need Another Hero (Thunderdome) topped the chart for six weeks.

Singles with the most weeks

28 weeks	*Cose Della Vita – Can't Stop Thinking Of You*
25 weeks	*Nutbush City Limits*
22 weeks	*The Best*
22 weeks	*GoldenEye*
21 weeks	*I Don't Wanna Fight*
19 weeks	*When The Heartache Is Over*
17 weeks	*What's Love Got To Do With It*
17 weeks	*We Don't Need Another Hero (Thunderdome)*
15 weeks	*Whatever You Want*
14 weeks	*Typical Male*

TINA IN THE UK

Tina has achieved 44 hit singles in the UK, which spent 302 weeks on the Top 100.

Tina's most successful singles are *River Deep – Mountain High* and *We Don't Need Another Hero (Thunderdome)*, which both peaked at no.3.

Singles with the most weeks

20 weeks	*River Deep – Mountain High*
18 weeks	*Nutbush City Limits*
16 weeks	*What's Love Got To Do With It*
14 weeks	*The Best*
13 weeks	*Let's Stay Together*
13 weeks	*We Don't Need Another Hero (Thunderdome)*
11 weeks	*I Don't Wanna Lose You*
10 weeks	*A Love Like Yours*
10 weeks	*GoldenEye*
9 weeks	*Private Dancer*
9 weeks	*I Don't Wanna Fight*
9 weeks	*Whatever You Want*

The Brit Certified/BPI (British Phonographic Industry) Awards

The BPI began certifying Silver, Gold & Platinum singles in 1973. From 1973 to 1988: Silver = 250,000, Gold = 500,000 & Platinum = 1 million. From 1989 onwards: Silver = 200,000, Gold = 400,000 & Platinum = 600,000. Awards are based on shipments, not sales; however, in July 2013 the BPI automated awards, based on actual sales since February 1994.

Gold	*The Best* (February 2019) = 400,000
Silver	*Let's Stay Together* (December 1983) = 250,000
Silver	*What's Love Got To Do With It* (August 1984) = 250,000
Silver	*We Don't Need Another Hero (Thunderdome)* (August 1985) = 250,000
Silver	*Proud Mary* (July 2017) = 200,000
Silver	*River Deep – Mountain High* (January 2020) = 200,000

TINA IN ZIMBABWE

Tina has achieved seven hit singles in Zimbabwe, which spent 54 weeks on the chart.

No.1 Singles

1974   *Nutbush City Limits*

Nutbush City Limits topped the chart for two weeks.

Singles with the most weeks

20 weeks   *Nutbush City Limits*
12 weeks   *We Don't Need Another Hero (Thunderdome)*
11 weeks   *What's Love Got To Do With It*
 5 weeks   *The Best*

All The Top 40 Albums

1 ~ RIVER DEEP – MOUNTAIN HIGH

River Deep – Mountain High/I Idolize You/A Love Like Yours (Don't Come Knocking Every Day/A Fool In Love/Make 'Em Wait/Hold On Baby/Save The Last Dance For Me/Oh Baby! (Things Ain't What They Used To Be/Every Day I Have To Cry/Such A Fool For You/It's Gonna Work Out Fine/You're So Fine

Produced by Ike Turner, except *River Deep – Mountain High, A Love Like Yours (Don't Come Knocking Everyday), Hold On Baby, Save The Last Dance For Me & Every Day I Have To Cry*, produced by Phil Spector.

USA: Philles Records PHLP-4011 (cancelled, 1966), A&M Records SP-4178 (1969).

RIVER DEEP – MOUNTAIN HIGH failed to enter the Top 100 of the Billboard 200 in 1969, however, it did spend eight weeks below no.100, peaking at no.102.

UK: London Records SHU 8298 (1966).

29.09.66: **27**

Australia
25.05.70: **29**

RIVER DEEP – MOUNTAIN HIGH, Ike & Tina's first album to enjoy Top 40 success, was recorded at the Gold Star studio in Los Angeles, California, with Ike producing seven of the 12 tracks, and Phil Spector producing the other five.

THE ULTIMATE TRUTH
IKE & TINA TURNER
RIVER DEEP ~ MOUNTAIN HIGH
PRODUCED BY PHIL SPECTOR
THE FIRST U.S. RELEASE OF ENGLAND'S CLASSIC BEST-SELLER
A&M / SP 4178

The release of *RIVER DEEP – MOUNTAIN HIGH* went ahead as planned in the UK, where the album charted for a solitary week at no.27. However, after the single *River Deep – Mountain High* bombed, the album was cancelled in the United States.

The liner notes of the UK release included a quote from Phil Spector: 'We can only assume that England is more appreciative of talent and exciting music than the U.S.'.

RIVER DEEP – MOUNTAIN HIGH was finally released outside the UK, including North America, in 1969. This reissued version of the album saw *You're So Fine* dropped, and replaced with *I'll Never Need More Than This* (placed after *Hold On Baby* on the running order).

The reissued *RIVER DEEP – MOUNTAIN HIGH* charted at no.29 in Australia, but struggled to no.102 on the Billboard 200 in the United States, and wasn't a hit anywhere else.

RIVER DEEP – MOUNTAIN HIGH produced two Top 40 singles:

- *River Deep – Mountain High*
- *A Love Like Yours (Don't Come Knocking Every Day)*

I'll Never Need More Than This, although it didn't feature on the album's original release, was released as a single in 1967, with Ike & Tina's cover of the 1960's Drifters hit *Save The Last Dance For Me* on the B-side.

I'll Never Need More Than This rose to no.15 on the 'bubbling under' section of the Hot 100 in the United States, but it failed to enter the Hot 100, and it wasn't a hit anywhere else.

2 ~ WORKIN' TOGETHER

Workin' Together/(As Long As I Can) Get You When I Want You/Get Back/The Way You Love Me/You Can Have It/Game Of Love/Funkier Than A Mosquita's Tweeter/Ooh Poo Pah Doo/Proud Mary/Goodbye, So Long/Let It Be

Produced by Ike Turner.

USA: Liberty LST-7650 (1970).

27.02.71: 52-48-30-27-27-27-30-27-**25**-32-53-58-56-70-82-99-96-96-100

UK: Liberty LBS 83455 (1970).

WORKIN' TOGETHER wasn't a hit in the UK.

Germany
15.04.71: peaked at no.**12**, charted for 20 weeks

Japan
25.02.71: peaked at no.**93**, charted for 2 weeks

WORKIN' TOGETHER was only the second Ike & Tina album to enjoy Top 40 success.
   In the United States, largely a result of the popularity of the Grammy-winning *Proud Mary*, the album gave the duo their biggest selling album to date, and rose to no.25 on the albums chart. The album did even better in Germany, where it achieved no.12, and it was also a minor hit in Japan.

Four singles were released from *WORKIN' TOGETHER*, but only the second single *Proud Mary* became a Top 40 hit anywhere.

The lead single from the album was the title track, which charted at no.41 on the Soul chart in the United States, but failed to enter the Hot 100. The album's third single, a cover of Jessie Hill's 1960 hit *Ooh Poo Pah Doo*, did enter the Hot 100, but it only climbed to no.60.

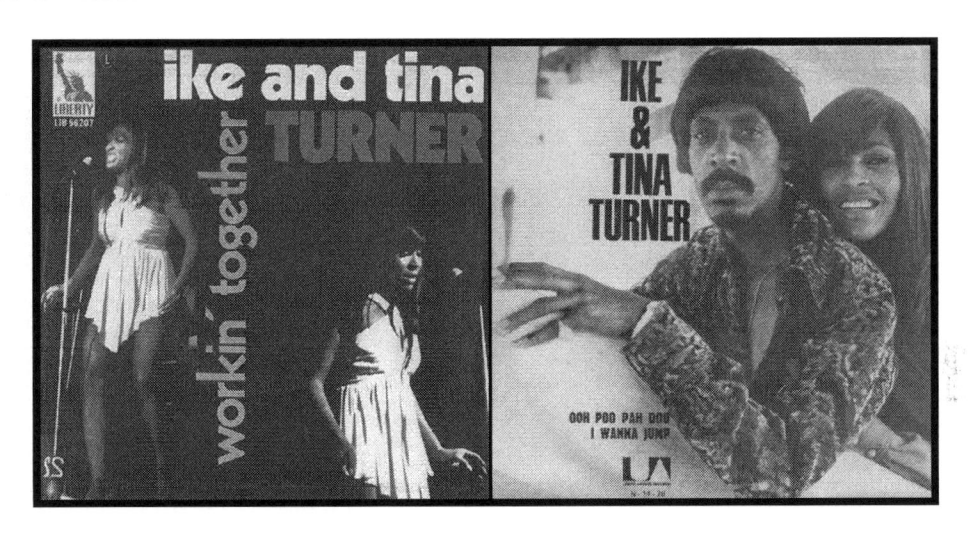

Ike & Tina recorded two Beatles hits for *WORKIN' TOGETHER*, *Get Back* and *Let It Be*, which were released as a single ~ with *Get Back* as the A-side ~ in a small number of countries, including France, Germany and Japan, but it wasn't a hit.

3 ~ WHAT YOU HEAR IS WHAT YOU GET – LIVE AT CARNEGIE HALL

LP1: *Introduction/Piece Of My Heart/Everyday People/Introduction To Tina/Doin' The Tina Turner/Sweet Soul Music/Ooh Poo Pah Doo/Honky Tonk Women/A Love Like Yours (Don't Come Knockin' Every Day)/Proud Mary/(Encore Of) Proud Mary*

LP2: *Proud Mary (Continued)/I Smell Trouble/Ike's Tune/I Want To Take You Higher/I've Been Loving You Too Long/Respect*

Produced by Ike Turner.

USA: United Artists Records UAS 9953 (1971).

10.07.71: 78-55-52-40-30-27-**25-25**-28-28-30-31-37-40-63-63-68-89

UK: United Artists Records UAD 60005/60006 (1971).

WHAT YOU HEAR IS WHAT YOU GET – LIVE AT CARNEGIE HALL wasn't a hit in the UK.

Australia
8.11.71: peaked at no.**38**, charted for 5 weeks

Japan
25.08.71: peaked at no.**71**, charted for 3 weeks

On 1st April 1971, with Fats Domino as their opening act, Ike & Tina played two concerts at New York City's Carnegie Hall. The second concert didn't finish until well past midnight.

Three months later, the double album *WHAT YOU HEAR IS WHAT YOU GET – LIVE AT CARNEGIE HALL* was released. Two tracks on the album, covers of Erma Franklin's 1967 hit *Piece Of My Heart* and Sly & The Family Stone's 1968 hit *Everyday People*, were performed by The Ikettes. The album also featured covers of *Sweet Soul Music*, *Honky Tonk Women* and *Respect*, which were big hits for Arthur Conley, the Rolling Stones and Aretha Franklin, respectively.

Like *WORKIN' TOGETHER*, *WHAT YOU HEAR IS WHAT YOU GET – LIVE AT CARNEGIE HALL* rose to no.25 in the United States. The album also achieved no.38 in Australia, and it was a minor hit in Japan.

WHAT YOU HEAR IS WHAT YOU GET – LIVE AT CARNEGIE HALL was reissued on CD in 1996 and 1999, and was digitally remastered and reissued on CD in 2012.

4 ~ LIVE IN PARIS – OLYMPIA 1971

LP1: *Grumbling/You Got Me Hummin'/Everyday People/Shake A Tail Feather/Medley (Gimme Some Lovin'/Sweet Soul Music)/Son Of A Preacher Man/Come Together/Proud Mary/A Love Like Yours Don't Come Knockin' Everyday*

LP2: *I Smell Trouble/Respect/Honky Tonk Women/I've Been Loving You Too Long/I Want To Take You Higher/Land Of 1000 Dances*

Produced by Eddie Adamis.

USA & UK: Not Released.

Germany: Liberty LBS 83468/69X (1971).

15.08.71: peaked at no.**25**, charted for 8 weeks

Another live double album, *LIVE IN PARIS – OLYMPIA 1971* was recorded at Ike & Tina's concert staged at Olympia, Paris, on 30th January 1971.
    Although this concert took place before the Carnegie Hall date, it wasn't released until August 1971, and it was only released in continental Europe.
    Like *WHAT YOU HEAR IS WHAT YOU GET – LIVE AT CARNEGIE HALL*, *LIVE IN PARIS – OLYMPIA 1971* was a mix of originals and covers, and a number of songs featured on both albums.
    LIVE IN PARIS – OLYMPIA 1971 charted at no.25 in Germany, but it wasn't a hit anywhere else.

5 ~ GOLD DISC

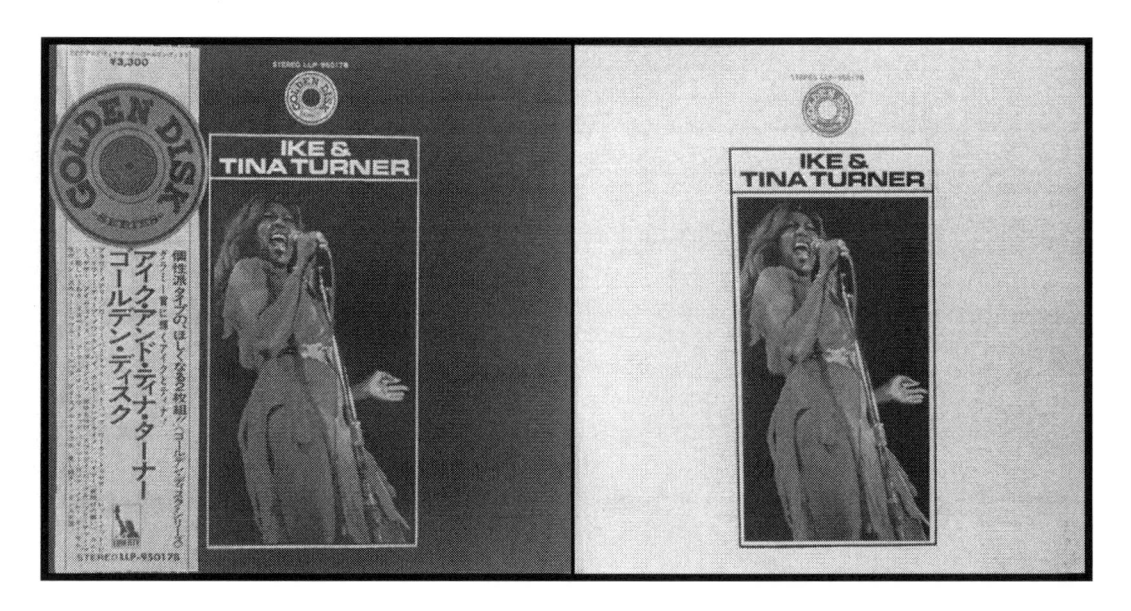

LP1: *Proud Mary/Ooh Poo Pah Doo/Get Back/Workin' Together/Let It Be/River Deep – Mountain High/Honky Tonk Women/I Want To Take You Higher/Come Together/I'm Yours/Up In Heah/Takin' Back My Name*

LP2: *Everyday People/Son Of A Preacher Man/Heard It Thru The Grapevine/Respect/A Fool In Love/Goodbye, So Long/Gimme Some Lovin' Medley/I Smell Trouble/I've Been Lovin' You Too Long/Land Of 1000 Dances*

Japan: Liberty LLP 95017B (1972).

5.06.72: peaked at no.**22**, charted for 10 weeks

Released exclusively in Japan, *GOLD DISC* was essentially a 'best of' compilation of Ike & Tina's hits and better known album tracks.
   A double album, *GOLD DISC* charted at no.22 and spent 10 weeks on the chart.

6 ~ NUTBUSH CITY LIMITS

Nutbush City Limits/Make Me Over/Drift Away/That's My Purpose/Fancy Annie/River Deep – Mountain High/Get It Out Of Your Mind/Daily Bread/You Are My Sunshine/Club Manhattan

Produced by Ike Turner.

USA: United Artists Records 7061 (1973).

NUTBUSH CITY LIMITS failed to enter the Top 100 of the Billboard 200, however, it did spend six weeks below no.100, peaking at no.163.

UK: United Artists Records UAS 29557 (1973).

NUTBUSH CITY LIMITS wasn't a hit in the UK.

Australia
24.03.75: peaked at no.**13**, charted for 46 weeks

Austria
15.02.74: **4-6-9** (monthly)

Germany
15.02.74: peaked at no.**21**, charted for 16 weeks

Italy
4.05.74: peaked at no.**4**, charted for 13 weeks

Spain
15.07.74: peaked at no.**23**, charted for 8 weeks

Ike wrote only two of the ten tracks he and Tina recorded for their *NUTBUSH CITY LIMITS* album, while Tina wrote five: *Nutbush City Limits*, *That's My Purpose*, *Fancy Annie*, *Daily Bread* and *Club Manhattan*. The latter was inspired by Manhattan Club, the nightclub in St. Louis, Illinois, where Tina and Ike first met.

The success of the album's title track as a single boosted *NUTBUSH CITY LIMITS* to no.4 in Austria and Italy, no.13 in Australia, no.21 in Germany and no.23 in Spain. The album was less successful in the United States, where it stalled at no.163, and it failed to chart at all in the UK.

The album included an alternate version of *River Deep – Mountain High*, which was issued as a single in France, but wasn't a hit.

NUTBUSH CITY LIMITS was released on CD for the first time in 2006.

In 1993, Tina re-recorded *Make Me Over* as *Tina's Wish*, for the soundtrack of her biopic, *What's Love Got To Do With It*.

ROBERT STIGWOOD présente
le nouveau film de
KEN RUSSELL
Tommy
the Movie
avec THE WHO
PRÉSENTÉ PAR
RTL
Tommy
Artemis Vintage Prints
Polydor
Robert Stigwood présente un film de Ken Russell
Tommy
avec The Who
avec
Oliver Reed Ann-Margret Roger Daltrey
dans le rôle de Tommy
et la participation de
Elton John
et avec Eric Clapton John Entwistle Keith Moon Paul Nicholas Jack Nicholson Robert Powell
Pete Townshend Tina Turner et The Who
producteur associé Harry Benn directeur musical Pete Townshend scénario de Ken Russell producteurs exécutifs Beryl Vertue et Christopher Stamp produit par Robert Stigwood et Ken Russell
réalisé par Ken Russell bande originale du film Polydor Records

TOMMY

Tina: *The Acid Queen*

Produced by The Who.

USA: Polydor PD 2-9502 (1975).

20.03.75: 97-50-27-18-14-8-7-3-3-**2**-3-3-4-6-7-9-11-15-23-23-30-44-41-48-69-89-77-77

UK: Polydor 2657104 (1975).

5.04.75: 32-**21-21**-22-25-35-41-49-37
2.08.75: 49-46-41-28-29-30-34-28-54-58-41-54-46-60

Australia
31.03.75: peaked at no.**6**, charted for 40 weeks

Germany
15.02.76: peaked at no.**50**, charted for 4 weeks

Italy
17.05.75: peaked at no.**7**, charted for 22 weeks

Netherlands
12.04.75: **11-11**-15-17-17-14-12-**11**-15-19

New Zealand
23.05.75: 11-6-8-7-12-19-22-22-14-6-6-**5**-8-6-10-11-17-13-18-20-26-19-32-32-31-33-39-25-37

Norway
4.11.75: **15**-x-x-16-19

Spain
28.07.75: peaked at no.**4**, charted for 64 weeks
4.02.07: 91

Tommy is a 1975 rock opera movie based on The Who's 1969 album with the same title.

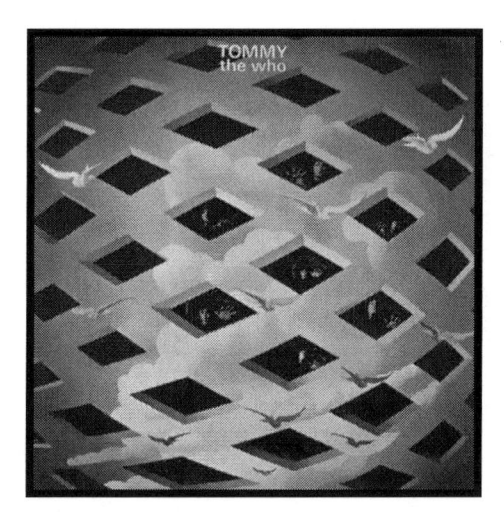

Tina was approached in 1974, and offered the role of the Acid Queen in the film.

'I was thrilled,' she wrote in her autobiography, *My Love Story*. 'Acting had been one of my ambitions when I was a child … I headed to London, where the film was being shot, certain I was on my way to becoming a movie star.'

As Ike was busy in Los Angeles at the time, Tina travelled alone.

'I felt like a bird who had escaped from a cage,' she admitted. 'I was so happy that Ike wasn't involved in any way.'

Tommy was directed by Ken Russell, and boosted a high profile cast that included:

- Roger Daltrey as Tommy Walker
- Ann-Margaret Olsson as Nora Walker
- Oliver Reed as Frank Hobbs
- Elton John as The Pinball Wizard
- Eric Clapton as The Preacher
- Keith Moon as Uncle Ernie

- Jack Nicholson as Dr A. Quackson (*aka* The Specialist)
- Paul Nicholas as Cousin Kevin
- The Who as themselves (during *Pinball Wizard*).

Tina's character, the Acid Queen, was a prostitute who also deals in LSD.

'It sounds crazy to say now,' she said, 'but at the time, I had no idea that the Acid Queen had any connection to drugs. So much for my wild and crazy life.'

Tommy cost $3 million to make, and premiered in March 1975; it took over $34 million at the box office.

The accompanying soundtrack album was a double, but Tina's only contribution was *The Acid Queen*.

TOMMY charted at no.2 in the United States, no.4 in Spain, no.5 in New Zealand, no.6 in Australia, no.7 in Italy, no.11 in the Netherlands, no.15 in Norway, no.21 in the UK and no.50 in Germany.

Tina
TURNER
Private Dancer
NEW ALBUM AND CASSETTE OUT NOW
FEATURES THE SMASH HITS "LET'S STAY TOGETHER" AND "HELP" AND INCLUDES THE NEW SINGLE "WHAT'S LOVE GOT TO DO WITH IT."
Capitol

7 ~ PRIVATE DANCER

USA/North American Edition: *I Might Have Been Queen/What's Love Got To Do With It/Show Some Respect/I Can't Stand The Rain/Better Be Good To Me/Let's Stay Together/1984/Steel Claw/Private Dancer*

UK/International Edition: *I Might Have Been Queen/What's Love Got To Do With It/Show Some Respect/I Can't Stand The Rain/Private Dancer/Let's Stay Together/Better Be Good To Me/Steel Claw/ Help/1984*

What's Love Got To Do With It, Show Some Respect & *I Can't Stand The Rain* produced by Terry Britten, *Let's Stay Together* & *1984* produced by Craig March & Martyn Ware, *Better Be Good To Me* & *I Might Have Been Queen* produced by Rupert Hine, *Private Dancer* & *Steel Claw* produced by John Carter, *Help* produced by Joe Sample, Ndugu Chancler & Wilton Felder.

USA: Capitol Records: C1 46041 (1984).

23.06.84: 57-36-29-24-22-18-13-9-8-4-4-4-4-4-**3**-4-**3**-**3**-**3**-**3**-**3**-**3**-**3**-**3**-**3**-**3**-4-4-5-5-6-8-8-9-11-10-9-9-9-6-5-5-5-5-7-8-10-15-16-18-18-21-22-24-28-28-32-36-42-45-45-42-39-33-33-33-40-42-43-51-56-55-52-50-56-73-83-95-x-91-91-91-92-100-95

UK: Capitol Records TINA 1 (1984).

30.06.84: 16-19-16-10-5-3-4-4-4-**2**-**2**-4-6-6-8-9-15-21-28-25-25-21-25-22-21-22-14-14-11-12-19-20-22-22-19-20-12-12-6-7-8-11-14-11-16-14-20-26-25-27-30-25-36-42-43-39-25-20-11-16-11-10-14-14-16-20-20-20-27-32-26-30-51-53-59-68-73-65-64-52-31-

26-24-26-27-26-33-40-45-46-43-62-66-77-78-76-97-78-x-99-81-67-73-63-76-67-82-76-85-66-72-75-72-63-64-66-57-54-62-64-79-69-92-83-76
10.01.87: 84-82-97-98-x-90-91-92
11.04.87: 98-x-x-62-71-85-73-88-86-89-69-53-89-79-92-x-97-91
11.08.90: 63
8.06.96: 79-89-90

Australia
23.07.84: peaked at no.**7**, charted for 74 weeks

Austria
15.11.84: 5-6-18-11-23-13-6-6-4-5-2-**1-1-1**-2-5-9-7-8-7-7-7-10-19-16-23-19-29 (bi-weekly)

Germany
18.06.84: 61-39-29-32-27-33-30-26-20-16-11-8-7-7-6-7-6-5-4-5-7-4-5-5-6-4-**2**-4-6-8-11-9-11-12-11-10-12-13-8-10-9-6-3-**2-2-2**-3-**2**-3-5-5-7-10-12-14-17-16-17-8-8-10-8-6-6-6-9-7-8-11-10-17-21-23-24-26-29-35-39-45-35-39-30-29-38-35-40-46-43-43-60-62-60-62-x-63

Japan
30.06.84: peaked at no.**46**, charted for 8 weeks

Netherlands
23.06.84: 28-22-32-40-33-50-x-x-42-30-19-8-8-**3-3**-7-8-5-6-5-**3**-6-9-9-10-13-13-13-19-14-20-16-17-19-23-24-31-34-36-36-33-37-33-29-19-19-22-33
3.08.85:45-44-28-22-28-41-34-36-41-46-39-46-45-x-x-64-64-x-x-75
15.03.86: 71-32-43-47-74

New Zealand
2.09.84: **2**-4-4-5-6-7-6-10-9-11-14-16-22-25-26-29-29-29-29-29-14-13-13-13-13-12-14-14-12-12-14-14-14-12-10-8-9-12-15-22-25-27-41-50-38-50-x-x-50-x-42-48-40-27-33-42-27-36-25-25-27-17-22-20-19-24-19-16-16-16-16-16-24-29-27-41-43-49

Norway
6.10.84: 11-14-**5-5-5**-10-10-11-14-15

South Africa
29.09.84: peaked at no.**5**, charted for 15 weeks

Spain
3.12.84: peaked at no.**7**, charted for 37 weeks

Sweden
12.06.84: 22-16-16-12-11-8-11-11-**7**-8-14-18-27-39-x-46-x-45 (bi-weekly)

Switzerland
10.06.84: 30-15-15-18-18-15-19-12-11-12-10-11-8-7-6-4-4-7-5-7-5-5-10-10-12-12-17-23-19-19-18-17-12-15-17-19-14-10-10-10-9-7-8-6-4-**3**-7-5-5-5-6-6-6-9-10-12-11-16-15-14-12-4-4-5-4-**3**-4-5-5-6-7-9-8-9-17-21-21-21-22-27-25-26-26-28-22-25-30-23

Zimbabwe
21.10.84: peaked at no.**2**

Tina released four solo albums between 1974 and 1979. One, *ACID QUEEN*, registered at no.115 on the Billboard 200 in the United States, but the other three ~ *TINA TURNS ON THE COUNTRY!*, *ROUGH* and *LOVE EXPLOSION* ~ all failed to chart anywhere.

The unexpected success of *Let's Stay Together* encouraged Tina and her manager Roger Davies, to think about a fifth solo album.

'Roger and I headed back to London, where I'd found support and inspiration from the earliest days of my career,' said Tina, 'starting with *River Deep – Mountain High*. The English people stepped up for me when America didn't. They never asked, "Where's Ike?". They accepted me as a solo artist.'

Let's Stay Together apart, Tina and Roger Davies started out with one song: *Better Be Good To Me*. A studio was booked, and Tina had just two and a half weeks to record the album that became *PRIVATE DANCER*, meaning Roger Davies dashed around London, frantically gathering potential songs for the album. As Tina commented: 'It was a funny way to begin a project.'

Including *Let's Stay Together*, Tina recorded ten songs for her fifth solo album. *Ball Of Confusion*, which Tina had recorded for B.E.F.'s 1982 album, *MUSIC OF QUALITY OF DISTINCTION VOLUME ONE*, wasn't included on the album. Nor was Tina's cover of Sam Cooke's *A Change Is Gonna Come*, which she had recorded at the same session as *Ball Of Confusion*. A remixed version of *A Change Is Gonna Come* was released on B.E.F.'s 1991 album, *MUSIC OF QUALITY AND DISTINCTION VOLUME 2*.

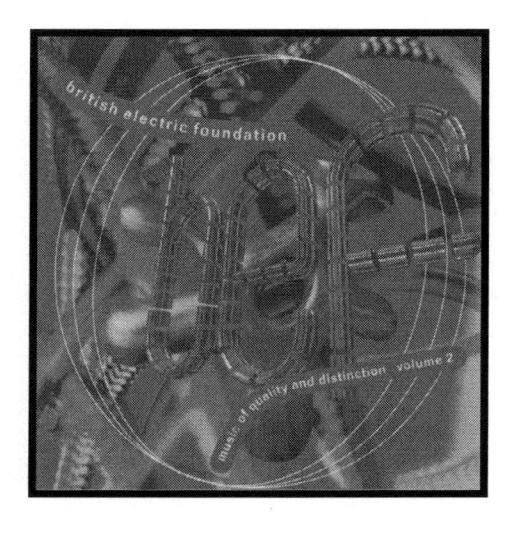

Tina Turner
PRIVATE DANCER
ALBUM
GOLD
PLATINUM
TRIPLE PLATINUM
Introducing the first hit of 1985...
PRIVATE DANCER
The TITLE TRACK from the Album.
SINGLE
SONY

Tina embraced the then relatively new MTV, by shooting music videos for each single released from the album.

'The one we did for *Private Dancer* was really ambitious,' she said, 'with fantasy sequences, dances choreographed by Arlene Phillips, five or six costume changes for me, and a wonderful location, the old Rivoli Ballroom in London.'

Tina also embarked on a 177 date Private Dancer Tour, to promote the album and the singles released from it. The tour launched in Helsinki, Finland, on 19th February 1985, and ended in Tokyo, Japan, on 28th December the same year.

An impressive seven of the ten (nine in North America) songs Tina recorded for *PRIVATE DANCER* became hit singles:

- *Let's Stay Together*
- *Help*
- *What's Love Got To Do With It*
- *Better Be Good To Me*
- *Private Dancer*
- *I Can't Stand The Rain*
- *Show Some Respect*

The album itself was a huge success, and easily eclipsed anything Tina had achieved as part of Ike & Tina Turner. The album hit no.1 in Austria, and achieved no.2 in Germany, New Zealand, the UK and Zimbabwe, no.3 in the Netherlands, Switzerland and the United States, no.5 in Norway and South Africa, and no.7 in Australia, Spain and Sweden.

At the 27th Annual Grammy Awards, staged at the Shrine Auditorium, Los Angeles, on 26th February 1985, *PRIVATE DANCER* picked up awards in four of the six categories where it was nominated:

- Record of the Year ~ *What's Love Got To Do With It*
- Song of the Year ~ *What's Love Got To Do With It*
- Best Pop Vocal Performance, Female ~ *What's Love Got To Do With It*
- Best Rock Vocal Performance, Female ~ *Better Be Good To Me*

Century Edition

PRIVATE DANCER was remastered and reissued in 1997, with seven bonus tracks:

- *I Wrote A Letter* (B-side of *Let's Stay Together*)
- *Rock'N'Roll Widow* (B-side of *Help*)
- *Don't Rush The Good Things* (B-side of *What's Love Got to Do With It*)
- *When I Was Young* (B-side of *Better Be Good To Me*)
- *What's Love Got To Do With It (Extended 12" Remix)*

- *Better Be Good To Me (Extended 12" Remix) (Edit)*
- *I Can't Stand The Rain (Extended 12" Remix*

30th Anniversary Edition

The 30th anniversary of *PRIVATE DANCER* was celebrated in 2015 ~ the album was remastered and reissued with a bonus CD that featured 15 tracks:

Ball Of Confusion (That's What The World Is Today)/I Wrote A Letter/Rock 'N' Roll Widow/Don't Rush The Good Things/When I Was Young/Keep Your Hands Off My Baby/Tonight (Live)/Let's Pretend We're Married (Live)/What's Love Got To Do With It (Extended 12" Remix)/Better Be Good To Me (Extended 12" Remix) (Edit)/I Can't Stand The Rain (Extended 12" Remix)/Show Some Respect (Extended Mix)/We Don't Need Another Hero (Thunderdome) (Single Edit)/One Of The Living (Single Remix)/It's Only Love

PRIVATE DANCER has sold an estimated 20+ million copies worldwide.

In 2020, *PRIVATE DANCER* was inducted into the Library of Congress's National Recording Registry in the United States, which honours recordings that are 'culturally, historically and aesthetically significant'.

8 ~ MAD MAX BEYOND THUNDERDOME

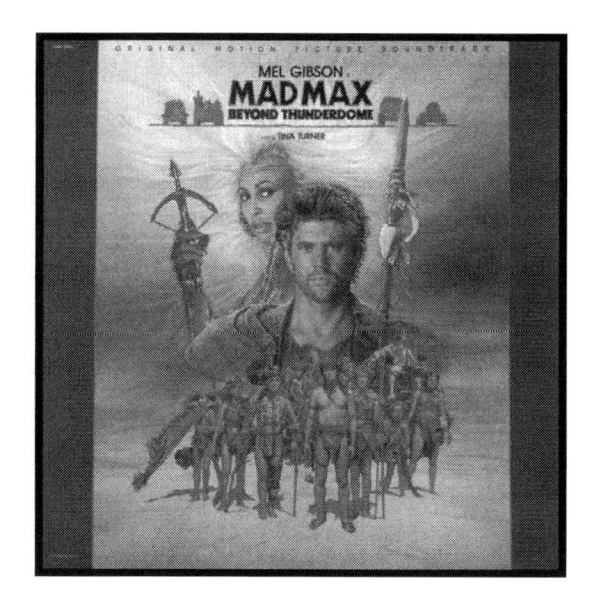

Tina: *We Don't Need Another Hero (Thunderdome)/One Of The Living/We Don't Need Another Hero (Thunderdome) (Instrumental)*

Maurice Jarre: *Bartertown/The Children/Coming Home*

USA: Capitol Records SWAV-12429 (1985).

24.08.85: 67-46-42-41-**39-39**-48-64-80-99

UK: Capitol Records EJ 24 0380 1 (1985).

MAD MAX BEYOND THUNDERDOME wasn't a hit in the UK.

Australia
19.08.85: peaked at no.**31**, charted for 13 weeks

Austria
15.09.85: 20-**17**-29-22-20 (bi-weekly)

Germany
19.08.85: 25-14-8-8-**7**-10-10-11-16-15-19-22-33-34-39-48-52-59

Italy
26.10.85: peaked at no.**19**, charted for 4 weeks

MAD MAX IS BACK!
"START QUEUING"
"...it is the most convincing and coherent fantasy environment since the megacities displayed in Scott's Blade Runner and Gilliam's Brazil ... one of the best movies of the year ... start queuing now. – NME.
"JUST MAD ABOUT MAX"
"Thrills all the way..." "... one of my films of the year..." – DAILY MAIL.
"ENTERTAINING"
"... highly enjoyable and much more thoughtful than most others in the genre ... very entertaining indeed..." – BBC 'FILM 85' – Barry Norman.
"MAX'LL DO NICELY"
"... more adult imagination, wit and ingenuity in any single frame of 'Thunderdome' than there is in the entire Spielberg oeuvre. Yes folks, we don't need another hero – 'Max'll do nicely.' – TIME OUT.
"TRUMPS"
"... director George Miller has come up trumps ..." – SOUNDS.
"EXPLOSIVE"
"Watch out, Rambo, Mad Max is back!" – THE SUN.
"TOTALLY BRILLIANT"
"... it's just totally brilliant ... (pause for breath) ... and ... well ... well, I'd go and see it if I were you." – SMASH HITS.
"POUNDING ADVENTURE"
"... two hours of pounding adventure that's enough to make even Indiana Jones sweat ..." – No 1.
"AMAZING"
"... it's brilliant." "... Tina Turner is amazing as Auntie Entity ..." "... I'd see it again (and again, and again)." "... Rambo go home: Max could blast him off the screen." – PENTHOUSE.
MEL GIBSON is MAD MAX BEYOND THUNDERDOME 15 starring TINA TURNER
KENNEDY MILLER Presents
MEL GIBSON TINA TURNER "MAD MAX BEYOND THUNDERDOME"
Music by MAURICE JARRE Director of Photography DEAN SEMLER A.C.S. Written by TERRY HAYES & GEORGE MILLER
Co-Produced by DOUG MITCHELL and TERRY HAYES Produced by GEORGE MILLER Directed by GEORGE MILLER and GEORGE OGILVIE
HEAR THE ORIGINAL SOUNDTRACK ALBUM ON CAPITOL RECORDS AND TAPES
NOW ACROSS LONDON AND ALL OVER THE COUNTRY

Netherlands
21.09.85: **50**

Spain
2.12.85: peaked at no.**6**, charted for 11 weeks

Switzerland
1.09.85: 9-8-**5**-8-11-7-11-8-11-15-25-28

Mad Max Beyond Thunderdome is a 1985 post-apocalyptic action/adventure film. It is the third film in the Mad Max franchise, and saw Mel Gibson returning once again to play the title character.

When the film's producers were discussing casting ideas for Aunty Entity, the ruthless queen of Bartertown who exiles Mad Max into the desert, they knew they wanted someone like Tina Turner, and even started calling Aunty Entity 'the Tina Turner character'.

'Finally,' said Tina, 'it occurred to someone to ask the real Tina if she would consider taking on the role.'

Having turned down a part in Steven Spielberg's *The Color Purple*, feeling the character she was offered was uncomfortably close to her life with Ike, Tina jumped at the chance to play Aunty Entity.

'The thought of travelling halfway around the world to the wilds of central Australia,' she said, 'shaving my head, wearing armour, and driving in fast cars, not to mention playing a queen … are you kidding? This was a dream come true.'

As well as Tina, *Mad Max Beyond Thunderdome* also starred:

- Mel Gibson as 'Mad' Max Rockatansky
- Bruce Spence as Jedediah the Pilot
- Adam Cockburn as Jedediah, Jr.
- Frank Thring as The Collector
- Angelo Rossitto as The Master
- Paul Larsson as Blaster
- Angry Anderson as Ironbar Bassey
- Robert Grubb as The Pig Killer
- Helen Buday as Savannah Nix
- Tom Jennings as Slake M'Thirst

The film was directed by George Miller and George Ogilvie, and cost around $10 to make. It premiered in July 1985, and took over $36 million at the box office in North America alone.

Tina recorded two new songs for the accompanying soundtrack album, and both were hits:

- *We Don't Need another Hero (Thunderdome)*
- *One Of The Living*

MAD MAX BEYOND THUNDERDOME charted at no.5 in Switzerland, no.6 in Spain, no.7 in Germany, no.17 in Austria, no.19 in Italy, no.31 in Australia, no.39 in the United States and no.50 in the Netherlands.

Deluxe Edition

In 2010, a 2CD deluxe edition titled *MAD MAX BEYOND THUNDERDOME – THE COMPLETE MOTION PICTURE SCORE* was released. This edition featured the film's complete score by Maurice Jarre and the Royal Philharmonic Orchestra, but due to licencing issues, Tina's *We Don't Need Another Here (Thunderdome)* and *One Of The Living* were omitted.

9 ~ BREAK EVERY RULE

Typical Male/What You Get Is What You See/Two People/Till The Right Man Comes Along/Afterglow/Girls/Back Where You Started/Break Every Rule/Overnight Sensation/ Paradise Is Here/I'll Be Thunder

Produced by Terry Britten except *Break Every Rule* & *I'll Be Thunder* by Rupert Hine, *Overnight Sensation* & *Paradise Is Here* by Mark Knopfler & Neil Dorfsman, *Back Where You Started* by Bryan Adams.

USA: Capitol Records PJ-12530 (1986).

27.09.86: 62-16-12-11-6-5-**4**-5-6-9-12-16-19-23-23-25-25-34-41-45-50-56-54-56-58-56-52-50-46-50-50-58-67-73-75-86-88-95-100

UK: Capitol Records EST 2018 (1986).

20.09.86: **2**-5-6-10-16-24-33-34-34-43-52-60-66-84-80-70-38-56-50-55-51-67-74-80-78-59-58-47-46-51-39-38-39-52-54-66-69-65-52-42-27-44-45-63-64-84-88-76-x-x-x-97

Australia
10.11.86: peaked at no.**11**, charted for 38 weeks

Austria
15.10.86: 8-3-4-3-5-14-8-7-9-18-14-18-11-10-11-4-**2**-5-4-4-6-13-10-13-26 (bi-weekly)

189

TINA!
—THE FIRST LADY OF ROCK—
Tina Turner "BREAK EVERY RULE"
tina turner
BREAK EVERY RULE
ティナは いつでもドラマティック!!
ブレイク・エヴリ・ルール
ティナ・ターナー
マスター・テープに限りなく近いミュージック・テープ
EXPANDED DYNAMIC RANGE
CD INFORMATION
TOSHIBA EMI

France
4.10.86: **16-16**-18-18 (bi-weekly)

Germany
15.09.86: 63-4-**1-1-1-1-1-1**-2-2-2-3-3-3-**1**-2-2-**1-1**-2-2-6-7-8-7-6-6-8-7-7-10-9-6-9-12-14-15-18-19-18-20-23-22-21-19-19-14-20-22-20-18-17-23-28-27-35-38-49-61-63

Italy
13.09.86: peaked at no.**7**, charted for 14 weeks

Japan
20.09.86: peaked at no.**41**, charted for 9 weeks

Netherlands
13.09.86: 53-8-**6**-8-7-9-11-13-13-21-26-25-28-35-40-49-39-47-68-x-66-59-44-27-23-18-19-32-37-31-27-29-32-50-58-66-x-x-66

New Zealand
23.11.86: 15-5-**4**-6-6-6-6-6-13-16-17-17-28-26-29-31-38-42-38-x-42-46-46-30-34-39-37

Norway
20.09.86: 5-**2-2-2**-3-3-5-6-7-9-14-15-19

South Africa
30.11.86: peaked at no.**20**, charted for 2 weeks

Spain
17.11.86: peaked at no.**1** (3), charted for 37 weeks

Sweden
24.09.86: **2-2**-3-7-14-17-19-17-20-25-38 (bi-weekly)

Switzerland
14.09.86: 11-2-2-**1-1**-2-2-3-2-3-4-3-7-8-13-10-11-9-10-12-16-14-15-21-20-22-19-16-19-20-23-9-11-11-12-23-24-30

Recorded during 1986, Tina's follow-up to her hugely successful *PRIVATE DANCER* album was released in September of the same year. And, while it couldn't quite match the sales of its predessessor, *BREAK EVERY RULE* was still a very success album.

Tina promoted *BREAK EVERY RULE* in much the same way as she had *PRIVATE DANCER*, with entertaining music videos and a lengthy Break Every Rule World Tour. The tour, which was sponsored by Pepsi, kicked off on 4th March 1987 in Munich, Germany, and originally it was billed as Tina's last tour.

'It is my last tour for now,' she stated. 'There probably won't be a tour with the next album because I want to devote some time to my movie career.'

The tour ran to the end of March 1988, ending in Osaka, Japan. On 16th January 1988, Tina played to an audience of 180,000+ at the Maracanã Stadium in Rio de Janeiro, Brazil, earning her a place in *Guinness World Records* for one of the largest concerts ever staged.

Eight of the 11 tracks Tina recorded for *BREAK EVERY RULE* were released as singles in one or more countries, with six achieving Top 40 status:

- *Typical Male*
- *Two People*
- *Girls*
- *What You Get Is What You See*
- *Break Every Rule*
- *Paradise Is Here*

The two exceptions were *Back Where You Started* and *Afterglow*.

Back Where You Started was only released as a 7" single in Canada, where it was a minor no.85 hit, and as a promotional 12" single in the United States, where it was ineligible to chart on the Hot 100. Tina did win another Grammy for *Back Where You Started*, for Best Rock Vocal Performance, Female.

Afterglow was issued as 12" single in the United States only. The single failed to enter the Hot 100, but it did rise to no.5 on Billboard's Dance Club Songs chart.

BREAK EVERY RULE was a global success, topping the chart for an impressive nine weeks in Germany. The album also hit no.1 in Spain and Switzerland, and achieved no.2 in Austria, Norway, Sweden and the UK, no.4 in New Zealand and the United States, no.6 in the Netherlands, no.7 in Italy, no.11 in Australia, no.16 in France, no.20 in South Africa and no.41 in Japan.

10 ~ TINA LIVE

Australia: *Addicted To Love/634-5789/A Change Is Gonna Come/In The Midnight Hour/ River Deep – Mountain High/Tonight/Let's Dance/Nutbush City Limits/Tearing Us Apart/ Let's Stay Together/It's Only Love/Land Of 1000 Dances/Proud Mary/Paradise Is Here*

Japan: *What You Get Is What You See/Break Every Rule/Typical Male/Two People/ Tonight/Let's Stay Together/Proud Mary/What's Love Got To Do With It/Tearing Us Apart/Private Dancer/Help/634-5789/Land Of 1000 Dances/It's Only Love/Paradise Is Here*

South America (Brazil): *What You Get Is What You See/Break Every Rule/Two People/ Tonight/Let's Stay Together/Proud Mary/What's Love Got To Do With It/Tearing Us Apart/Help/Land Of 1000 Dances/It's Only Love/Paradise Is Here*

Produced by John Hudson & Terry Britten.

USA & UK: Not Released.

Australia: Interfusion RML 53257 (1987).

11.01.88: peaked at no.**37**, charted for 11 weeks

New Zealand
28.02.88: **27**-33-34-43

TINA LIVE was released in Australasia, Japan and South America instead of *LIVE IN EUROPE*, to promote Tina's Break Every Rule World Tour and *BREAK EVERY RULE* album. The track listing varied from country to country, as did the album's sleeve design.

TINA LIVE formed part one of a two record release, with part two ~ simply titled *MORE LIVE!* ~ following later in 1988.

TINA LIVE charted at no.27 in New Zealand and no.37 in Australia.

11 ~ TINA LIVE IN EUROPE

LP1: *What You Get Is What You See/Break Every Rule/I Can't Stand The Rain/Two People/Typical Male/Better Be Good To Me/Addicted To Love/Private Dancer/We Don't Need Another Hero (Thunderdome)/What's Love Got To Do With It/Let's Stay Together/Show Some Respect*

LP2: *Land Of 1000 Dances/In The Midnight Hour/634-5789/A Change Is Gonna Come/Tearing Us Apart/Help/Tonight/Let's Dance/It's Only Love/Nutbush City Limits/Paradise Is Here*

CD Bonus Tracks: *Girls/Back Where You Started/River Deep – Mountain High/Overnight Sensation*

Produced by John Hudson & Terry Britten.

USA: Capitol Records C1 590126 (1988).

23.04.88: 88-**86-86**

UK: Capitol Records ESTD 1 (1988).

2.04.88: **8**-9-12-21-22-35-42-55-56-68-87-80-80

Australia
4.10.93: peaked at no.**79**, charted for 5 weeks

Austria
15.04.88: 6-**4-4**-16-16-25-30-14-22 (bi-weekly)

Germany
4.04.88: 9-**4-4**-5-5-8-11-11-15-16-19-22-27-32-33-37-51-59-64

Italy
2.04.88: peaked at no.**18**, charted for 7 weeks

Japan
25.02.88: peaked at no.**87**, charted for 3 weeks

Netherlands
9.04.88: 20-10-10-18-20-21-24-45-46-61-73
18.02.89: **6-6**-10-10-12-14-17-23-22-28-37-39-37-37-38-49-54-74-84-98

New Zealand
17.10.93: **46**

Norway
9.04.88: 17-17-**16**-x-20-20-20
16.02.08: 35

Spain
16.05.88: peaked at no.**18**, charted for 14 weeks

Sweden
30.03.88: 25-**8**-10-17-32 (bi-weekly)

Switzerland
3.04.88: 17-8-**3**-6-5-10-10-13-22-25-27-19

LIVE IN EUROPE was Tina's first live album as a solo artist. Released in two parts as *TINA LIVE* and *MORE TINA!* in Australasia, Japan and South America, *LIVE IN EUROPE* was recorded during Tina's Break Every Rule World Tour, Private Dancer Tour and *Tina Turner: Break Every Rule* TV Special, at five different venues:

- National Exhibition Centre, Birmingham, England
- Camden Palace, London, England
- Wembley Arena, London, England
- Westfallenhalle, Dortmund, West Germany
- Isstadion, Stockhol, Sweden

Four of the five singles released from *LIVE IN EUROPE* achieved Top 40 status in one or more countries:

- *Nutbush City Limits*
- *Addicted To Love*
- *Tonight*
- *634-5789*

The one exception was Tina's live performance of Sam Cooke's *A Change Is Gonna Come*, which was released as a single in Europe, but wasn't a hit anywhere.

Let's Dance, featuring covers of hits by Chris Montez and David Bowie, which Tina performed live with David Bowie at the NEC, Birmingham, on 23rd March 19985, was belatedly a no.31 hit in France in 2016, on the strength of streaming and digital sales..

LIVE IN EUROPE sold better than many live albums do, charting at no.3 in Switzerland, no.4 in Austria and Germany, no.6 in the Netherlands, no.8 in Sweden and the UK, no.16 in Norway, and no.18 in Italy and Spain. However, the album was only a minor success in the United States and Japan,

Tina won a Grammy Award for *LIVE IN EUROPE*, for Best Rock Vocal Performance, Female.

tina turner

foreign affair

Tina Turner is back with her best album yet

This new studio recording includes the hit single "The Best" and collaborations with many artists including Mark Knopfler, Tommy Joe White, Mike Chapman, Holly Knight, Albert Hammond, Graham Lyle & Dan Hartman.

The worldwide release date is Monday 18th September

COMPACT DISC   CASSETTE   RECORD

12 ~ FOREIGN AFFAIR

Steamy Windows/The Best/You Know Who (Is Doing You Know What)/Undercover Agent For The Blues/Look Me In The Heart/Be Tender With Me Baby/You Can't Stop Me Loving You/Ask Me How I Feel/Falling Like Rain/I Don't Wanna Lose You/Not Enough Romance/Foreign Affair

Produced by Dan Hartman except *The Best* & *Ask Me How I Feel* co-produced by Tina, *Falling Like Rain* produced by Rupert Hine, *I Don't Wanna Lose You* produced by Roger Davies, Albert Hammond & Graham Lyle, *Foreign Affair* produced by Roger Davies & Tony Joe White.

USA: Capitol Records C1 91873 (1989).

7.10.89: 86-36-35-**31-31**-36-43-50-48-48-51-60-60-71-71-75-79

UK: Capitol Records ESTU 2103 (1989).

30.09.89: **1**-2-2-3-8-14-20-22-26-23-11-4-3-3-5-4-3-5-9-14-12-11-8-6-5-10-10-15-24-20-24-26-29-30-33-27-26-23-26-32-36-33-39-32-22-12-13-12-12-11-14-18-11-12-16-17-19-26-26-32-48-52-49-46-49-42-47-57-49-59-73-56-72-64-0-72-73-73-74
8.06.96: 85-90-94

Australia
16.10.89: peaked at no.**14**, charted for 46 weeks

Austria
1.10.89: 22-**1**-2-**1**-2-**1**-(bi-weekly to here)-**1**-**1**-5-5-6-5-4-6-6-8-7-8-7-8-11-12-11-12-18-17-16-14-13-14-9-6-7-11-11-13-11-18-20-16-17-17-18-14-20-23-25

France
4.01.90: 29-30-31-**27**-28-40-x-40-39-38-42-37-48-39-36-45-43 (bi-weekly)

Germany
2.10.89: **1**-**1**-**1**-**1**-3-3-3-4-5-7-7-8-9-12-8-10-13-10-7-9-9-11-7-8-7-7-13-13-14-16-18-19-20-18-18-15-15-19-14-17-18-19-22-22-25-23-32-32-33-35-38-48-50-49-63-65-68-64-65-66-72-74-69-72

Italy
23.09.89: peaked at no.**2**, charted for 35 weeks

Netherlands
30.09.89: 72-18-13-10-**9**-10-15-21-23-30-38-42-51-75-87-89-77-65-61-61-57-52-55-55-40-36-34-35-38-47-49-62-70-77-x-x-x-92-75-64-52-46-44-38-32-37-45-45-56-61-69-75-83-93

New Zealand
12.11.89: 21-35-38-x-x-25-25-25-25-35-16-**7**-14-11-17-21-21-28-37-31-39

Norway
30.09.89: 6-**1**-**1**-2-2-2-**1**-2-2-5-4-5-8-10-10-10-7-7-12-12-15

South Africa
12.10.89: peaked at no.**1** (10), charted for 32 weeks

Spain
2.10.89: peaked at no.**8**, charted for 30 weeks

Sweden
4.10.89: **1**-**1**-3-3-8-12-12-12-17-20-27-40-x-50-x-x-49-35 (bi-weekly)

Switzerland
1.10.89: **1**-**1**-**1**-**1**-**1**-**1**-**1**-**1**-**1**-2-**1**-2-2-2-2-2-2-3-4-3-6-8-7-6-5-9-16-17-14-16-13-21-26-28-22-26-26-24-19-8-8-9-15-19-17-27-26-27-29-31-34

Zimbabwe
18.11.90: peaked at no.**4**

FOREIGN AFFAIR was Tina's seventh studio album as a solo artist, and continued her impressive run of success, selling especially well in Europe.

For the first time in her solo career, Tina was credited as co-producing two songs she recorded for one of her albums, namely *The Best* and *Ask Me How I Feel*. *The Best* went on to become one of her signature songs, and was one of four songs Holly Knight co-wrote for *FOREIGN AFFAIR*.

'Tina called me to say she was in town.' said Holly Knight, 'that she loved the new bridge to *The Best*, and asked if I had any other tunes to play her. I threw four tunes on a cassette and went to visit her in her hotel. She picked three of the tunes and said she wanted to record all three. I had to pinch myself, this would make six tunes of mine she had cut to date, and I was overjoyed.'

As well as *The Best*, the songs Holly Knight contributed were *Be Tender With Me Baby*, *You Can't Stop Me Loving You* and *Ask Me How I Feel*.

Although she had indicated her Break Every Rule World Tour would be her last, Tina embarked on another tour to promote *FOREIGN AFFAIR*. The tour was originally billed as Foreign Affair: The Farewell Tour, and opened on 27th April 1990 in Antwerp, Belgium. Tina played 121 dates, all of them in Europe, ending the tour on 4th November 1990 in Rotterdam, the Netherlands.

'I've always thought this would be the final one,' Tina reflected, after the tour, 'but I must admit I now have mixed feelings. I'm the first woman to fill all these stadiums and the feeling from all those fans night after night was fantastic. I don't want to close that door completely.

Six of the 12 songs Tina recorded for *FOREIGN AFFAIR* were released as singles, and all six achieved Top 40 status in at least one country:

- *The Best*
- *I Don't Wanna Lose You*
- *Steamy Windows*
- *Foreign Affair*
- *Look Me In The Heart*
- *Be Tender With Me Baby*

FOREIGN AFFAIR gave Tina her first no.1 album in the UK, and topped the chart in both South Africa and Switzerland for an impressive 10 weeks. The album also went to no.1 in Austria, Germany and Norway, and charted at no.2 in Italy, no.4 in Zimbabwe, no.7 in New Zealand, no.8 in Spain, no.9 in the Netherlands, no.14 in Australia and no.27 in France.

The album was less well received in the United States, where it only rose to no.31 on the Billboard 200 album chart.

Tina was nominated for a Grammy for *FOREIGN AFFAIR*, for Best Rock Vocal Performance, Female, but the award went to Bonnie Raitt, for *NICK OF TIME*.

Tina Turner
simply the best

It's a long road from star to superstar but Tina Turner has made it look easy.

Four multi-platinum albums, including 1984's Grammy-winning Record of the Year *Private Dancer*. Worldwide record sales over 25 million. Two #1 singles. And the #1 international tour of 1990.

Now Tina brings you **Simply The Best.**

Fifteen of her greatest hits featuring *"What's Love Got To Do With It," "Private Dancer," "River Deep–Mountain High"* and a fresh version of her classic *"Nutbush City Limits,"* plus three brand-new tracks including the first single and video *"Love Thing"* and *"I Want You Near Me."* A total of eighteen songs, over 70 minutes of music.

And it doesn't stop there. Look for the companion home video, **Simply The Best: The Video Collection**, available on Capitol Home Video November 19.

Tina gives you nothing less than **Simply The Best**...
ON CAPITOL COMPACT DISCS, CASSETTES AND HOME VIDEOS.

13 ~ SIMPLY THE BEST

USA: *The Best/Better Be Good To Me/I Can't Stand The Rain/What's Love Got To Do With It/I Don't Wanna Lose You/Nutbush City Limits (The 90s Version)/What You Get Is What You See/Let's Stay Together/River Deep – Mountain High/Steamy Windows/Typical Male/We Don't Need Another Hero (Thunderdome)/Private Dancer/Look Me In The Heart/It Takes Two* (& Rod Stewart)/*I Want You Near Me/Way Of The World/Love Thing*

UK: *The Best/What's Love Got To Do With It/I Can't Stand The Rain/I Don't Wanna Lose You/Nutbush City Limits (The 90s Version)/Let's Stay Together/Private Dancer/We Don't Need Another Hero (Thunderdome)/Better Be Good To Me/River Deep – Mountain High/Steamy Windows/Typical Male/It Takes Two (& Rod Stewart)/Addicted To Love (Live)/Be Tender With Me Baby/I Want You Near Me/Way Of The World/Love Thing*

USA: Capitol Records CDP 7 97152 2 (1991).

SIMPLY THE BEST failed to enter the Top 100 of the Billboard 200, however, it did spend 17 weeks outside the Top 100, peaking at no.113.

UK: Capitol Records CDESTV 1 (1991).

12.10.91: 3-**2**-4-**2**-3-7-8-7-6-4-5-4-3-**2**-4-5-6-8-9-15-18-9-8-12-12-10-20-21-14-25-27-31-
37-35-34-40-40-28-38-50-48-44-43-49-47-45-52-61-60-64-77-57-76-73-86-91-82-88-
69-70-70-48-34-32-32-37-38-47-60-59-63-72-90-93-97-93-78-x-x-x-x-99-92-x-99-33-
32-39-44-45-61-52-74-64-92-76-52-59-47-61-78-71-75-97-81-68-62-65-74-65-72-73-
68-69-71-64-51-62-43-51-54-65-83-65-79-81-92-62-66-67-86-91-84
9.07.94: 100-x-x-87-73-75-71-85-94-88-14-9-13-16-19-27-30-35-48-91-x-x-x-x-88-81-

39-43-48-51-63-73-92-x-x-x-x-x-x-x-x-48-31-36-35-29-49-30-55-59-64-x-x-83-84-x-x-x-x-96-94
23.03.96: 95
18.05.96: 92-92-90-x-x-87-96-x-58-67-55-55-64-62-67-87-92-88
8.03.97: 96-60-57-66-78-98-x-56-76-96-x-99
25.10.97: 99
14.03.98: 83-x-93

Australia
4.11.91: peaked at no.**11**, charted for 77 weeks

Austria
13.10.91: 17-**8-8**-19-11-11-13-16-11-15-16-16-13-11-10-11-14-13-12-11-15-13-14-15-16-21-24

Belgium
23.03.96: 44-38-x-44-41
1.06.96: 32-25-34-29-35-x-44-47-x-x-43-35-42-46-x-33-**23**-38
5.08.00: 46-37-43

Finland
17.08.96: **19**-32
5.08.00: 34-**19**

Germany
14.10.91: 12-10-6-5-**4-4**-5-6-8-8-9-6-9-11-10-12-14-14-20-18-17-21-26-21-26-38-39-38-41-44-46-50-62-69-72-74-74-69-78-79
3.02.97: 87-58-56-61-63-50-78-100-99-82-96

Italy
5.10.91: peaked at no.**5**, charted for 19 weeks

Netherlands
12.10.91: 22-8-7-**5-5**-9-10-12-12-13-12-x-16-18-20-17-16-12-10-10-8-6-10-11-13-16-22-25-28-36-55-66-70-74-85-92-96-92-81-62-54-46-39-32-33-33-35-40-43-47-50-66-47-61-78-89-92
4.09.93: 98-77-63-67-88-98-93-97
18.12.93: 92-79-74-55-53-85-90-86-89-91-91-99-89-83-93
4.10.97: 56-86
29.07.00: 88-84-88

New Zealand
17.11.91: **1-1**-2-3-4-4-4-4-4-3-11-8-9-9-13-17-26-18-39-29-30-20-18-17-21-12-14-17-20-17-14-18-17-24-19-22-20-19-30-22-34-25-43-36-31-32-39-31-40-30-44-22-21-37-41

24.01.93: 45-x-50
1.08.93: 41-45-x-50-x-43-40-35-16-10-5-6-3-3-3-3-9-13-17-25-25-25-27-40-35-45-47
30.03.97: 45-30-26-19-19-33-41-39

Norway
12.10.91: 16-8-8-**6**-7-10-14-15-13-20-x-19-19-19-19-10-14-8-9-9-9-14-x-19
5.08.00: 33-19-27

South Africa
26.10.91: peaked at no.**1** (2), charted for 29 weeks

Spain
18.11.91: peaked at no.**11**, charted for 26 weeks

Sweden
9.10.91: 41-10-**5-5**-11-12-16-19-24-30-31 (bi-weekly)
16.08.96: 53
10.08.01: 51

Switzerland
13.10.91: 8-16-7-12-8-**3**-6-8-9-23-20-20-13-16-16-18-22-20-26-23-40
1.12.19: 97-96

Zimbabwe
29.06.92: peaked at no.**5**

SIMPLY THE BEST was Tina's first greatest hits compilation album as a solo artist and, given her success since she released *Let's Stay Together*, she had a wealth of material to choose from.

The compilation included three new songs, plus a re-recorded dance version of *Nutbush City Limits*, which was sub-titled 'The 90s Version). The three new songs were:

- *Way Of The World*
- *Love Thing*
- *I Want You Near Me*

Nutbush City Limits (The 90s Version) and the three new songs were all released as singles, and all four achieved Top 40 status in one or more countries.

In Australasia, a limited edition of *SIMPLY THE BEST* was released with a bonus 5-track CD that featured:

- *(Simply) The Best*
- *I'm A Lady*
- *I Can't Stand The Rain (Extended 12" Remix)*
- *Be Tender With Me Baby*
- *Show Some Respect*

I'm A Lady was a new song, while *(Simply) The Best* was a new version of *The Best*, which Tina re-recorded as a duet with Australian rocker Jimmy Barnes. The latter was issued as a single in Australia and New Zealand, where it became a hit, and *I'm A Lady* was released as the B-side of *Love Thing* in most countries.

SIMPLY THE BEST hit no.1 in New Zealand and South Africa, and charted at no.2 in the UK, no.3 in Switzerland, no.4 in Germany, no.5 in Italy, the Netherlands, Sweden and Zimbabwe, no.6 in Norway, no.8 in Austria, no.11 in Australia and Spain, no.19 in Finland and no.23 in Belgium.

In the United States, where compilations often disappoint chart-wise, *SIMPLY THE BEST* struggled to no.113 on the Billboard 200, but failed to enter the Top 100.

14 ~ WHAT'S LOVE GOT TO DO WITH IT

USA: *I Don't Wanna Fight/Rock Me Baby/Disco Inferno/Why Must We Wait Until Tonight?/Nutbush City Limits/(Darlin') You Know I Love You/Proud Mary/A Fool In Love/It's Gonna Work Out Fine/Stay Awhile/I Might Have Been Queen/What's Love Got To Do With It*

UK: *I Don't Wanna Fight/Rock Me Baby/Disco Inferno/Why Must We Wait Until Tonight?/Stay Awhile/Nutbush City Limits/(Darlin') You Know I Love You/Proud Mary/A Fool In Love/It's Gonna Work Out Fine/Shake A Tail Feather/I Might Have Been Queen/What's Love Got To Do With It/Tina's Wish*

USA: Virgin Records 0777-7-88189-2-2 (1993).

3.07.93: 32-21-**17-17**-19-22-27-31-35-37-39-44-45-47-73-92-100

UK: Parlophone CDPCSD 128 (1993).

19.06.93: **1**-2-5-7-11-14-22-18-20-10-11-10-13-19-28-27-31-30-30-36-26-28-33-35-40-46-48-47-40-43-57-62-68-97

Australia
2.08.93: peaked at no.**31**, charted for 17 weeks

Austria
20.06.93: 37-39-15-13-**6**-15-9-19-21-18-32-14-20-27-22-14-21-32

France
27.06.93: **21**-32-**21**-25-29-42-42-44-47-37-49-54-59-64-69-74-79-44-48-94

Germany
21.06.93: 28-24-**8-8**-10-12-13-16-18-23-25-24-24-24-27-23-31-36-39-45-59-77-75

Italy
19.06.93: peaked at no.**9**, charted for 20 weeks

Netherlands
19.06.93: 60-25-17-**12-12**-20-23-24-29-34-39-41-43-45-45-71
27.11.93: 69-54-46-37-32-40-50-60-56-57-70

New Zealand
27.06.93: 40-10-**6**-8-13-10-20-17-42-23-36-x-41-36-31-23-22-41-47-17-16-8-9-14-24-31-x-x-x-50

Norway
12.06.93: 13-**6**-7-9-12-12-12-17

South Africa
6.11.93: peaked at no.**18**, charted for 2 weeks

Spain
1.11.93: peaked at no.**17**, charted for 20 weeks

Sweden
30.06.93: **22**-27-37-39-x-33-34-29-30-34-46-(bi-weekly to here)-x-47-41-49

Switzerland
20.06.93: 18-23-**5**-7-6-8-10-12-13-15-13-10-8-9-12-9-13-8-12-13-16-19-27-31-37-37

Zimbabwe
1.11.93: peaked at no.**5**

What's Love Got To Do With It is a 1993 biopic which tells 'The True Life Story of Tina Turner'. The screenplay for the film was written by Kate Lanier, based on the 1986 memoir *I, Tina – My Life Story*, which Kurt Loder wrote with Tina. The film was directed by Brian Gibson.

A number of high profile singers/actors were considered, to play the part of Tina in the biopic, including Halle Berry, Janet Jackson, Vanessa Williams and Whitney Houston. Whitney was actually offered the part but, aside from the fact she was pregnant at the time, she wasn't really interested in playing another artist who was still alive and active.

Angela Bassett secured the part of Tina just one month before production of the biopic began production in December 1992. In this short time, she had to learn to talk, move and dance like Tina, and given more time she would have loved to have a go at singing her part as well.

'I did think about it for a second, though,' she admitted, but given how little time she had it just wasn't realistic.

As well as Angela Bassett as Anna Mae Bullock/Tina Turner, *What's Love Got To Do With It* starred:

- Laurence Fishburne as Ike Turner
- Rae'Ven Larrymore Kelly as Anna Mae Bullock (young)
- Cora Lee Day as Grandma Georgina
- Jenifer Lewis as Zelma Bullock
- Phyllis Yvonne Stickney as Alline Bullock
- Khandi Alexander as Darlene
- Penny Johnson Jerald as Lorraine Taylor
- Vanesa Bell Calloway as Jackie
- Bo Kane as Dance Show Host
- James Reyne as Roger Davies
- Rob LaBelle as Phil Spector
- Suli McCullough as Craig Turner
- Damon Hines as Ronnie Turner
- Richard T. Jones as Ike Turner, Jr. (young)
- Elijah B. Saleem as Ike Turner, Jr. (teenage)
- Shavar Ross as Michael Turner

Laurence Fishburne turned down the part of Ike five times, feeling the biopic was very one-sided, and that Ike was 'obviously the villain of the piece, but there was no explanation as to why he behaved the way he behaved, why she (Tina) was with him for sixteen to twenty years, what made her stay.'

Only after some changes were made, giving at least some insight into Ike's behaviour, did he finally accept the role ~ citing, at the same time, the casting of Angela Bassett as Tina was the deciding factor.

Tina re-recorded all the Ike & Tina songs featured in the biopic, with Laurence Fishburne singing Ike's parts on *It's Gonna Work Out Fine* and *Proud Mary*. Original masters were used for her post-Ike recordings and *River Deep – Mountain High*, with Angela Bassett lip-syncing Tina's vocals.

In her screenplay for *What's Love Got To Do With It*, Kate Lanier toned down or completely deleted much of the brutally Tina suffered at the hands of Ike, as revealed in *I, Tina – My Life Story*. This, the way she was portrayed as a woman who was a victim to a con man and the fact parts were fictionalised, meant Tina wasn't happy with certain aspects of the finished biopic.

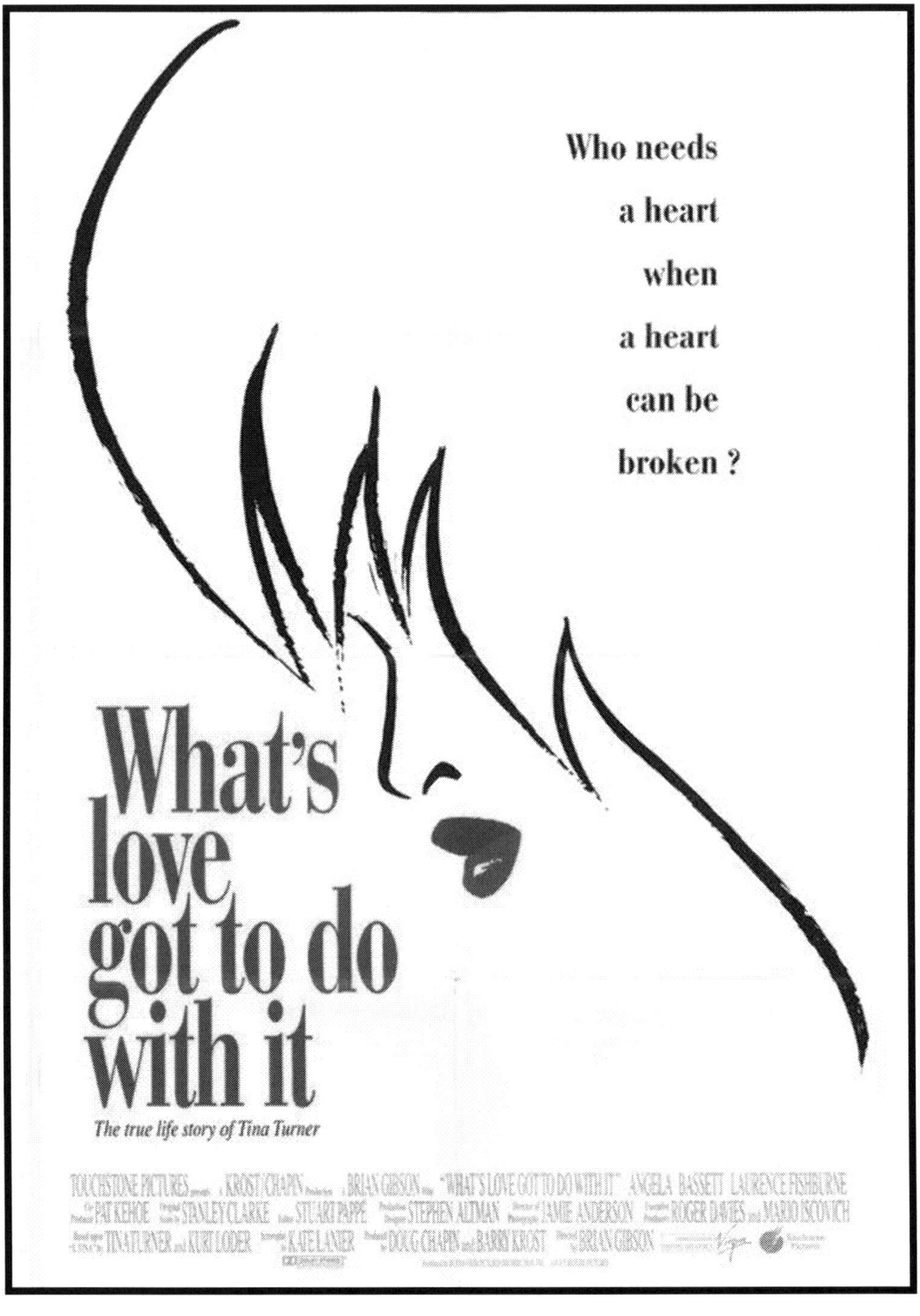
Who needs
a heart
when
a heart
can be
broken ?
What's love got to do with it
The true life story of Tina Turner
TOUCHSTONE PICTURES KROST/CHAPIN BRIAN GIBSON "WHAT'S LOVE GOT TO DO WITH IT" ANGELA BASSETT LAURENCE FISHBURNE
PAT KEHOE STANLEY CLARKE STUART PAPPÉ STEPHEN ALTMAN JAMIE ANDERSON ROGER DAVIES MARIO ISCOVICH
TINA TURNER KURT LODER KATE LANIER DOUG CHAPIN BARRY KROST BRIAN GIBSON

'How weak! How shallow! How dare you think that was what I was?' she asked in one interview. 'I was in control every minute there. I was there because I wanted to be, because I had promised. OK, so if I was a victim, fine. Maybe I was a victim for a short while. But give me credit for thinking the whole time I was there. See, I do have pride.'

What's Love Got To Do With It cost $15 million to make, and premiered in June 1993 to critical acclaim ~ the biopic took over $39 million at the box office.

Angela Bassett won a Golden Globe, for Best Performance by an Actress in a Motion Picture, for her portrayal of Tina. She was also nominated for an Academy Award, for Best Actress in a Leading Role, and her co-star Laurence picked up a nomination for Best Actor in a Leading Role, but neither won.

Tina recorded three new songs for *What's Love Got To Do With It*:

- *I Don't Wanna Fight*
- *Disco Inferno*
- *Why Must We Wait Until Tonight?*

All three were included on the accompanying soundtrack album, and became hit singles. The new version of *Proud Mary*, recorded by Tina with Laurence Fishburne, was also issued as a single but it wasn't a hit.

Pos	LW	Title, Artist		Peak Pos	WoC
1	New	WHAT'S LOVE GOT TO DO WITH IT TINA TURNER	PARLOPHONE	1	1
2	2	AUTOMATIC FOR THE PEOPLE REM	WARNER BROTHERS	1	37
3	1↓	NO LIMITS 2 UNLIMITED	PWL CONTINENTAL	1	5
4	7↑	POCKET FULL OF KRYPTONITE THE SPIN DOCTORS	EPIC	4	7

The *WHAT'S LOVE GOT TO DO WITH IT* soundtrack gave Tina her second no.1 album in the UK, and sold well in most countries, charting at no.5 in Switzerland and Zimbabwe, no.6 in Austria, New Zealand and Norway, no.8 in Germany, no.9 in Italy, no.12 in the Netherlands, no.17 in Spain and the United States, no.18 in South Africa, no.21 in France, no.22 in Sweden and no.31 in Australia.

Tina
wildest
dreams
Turner

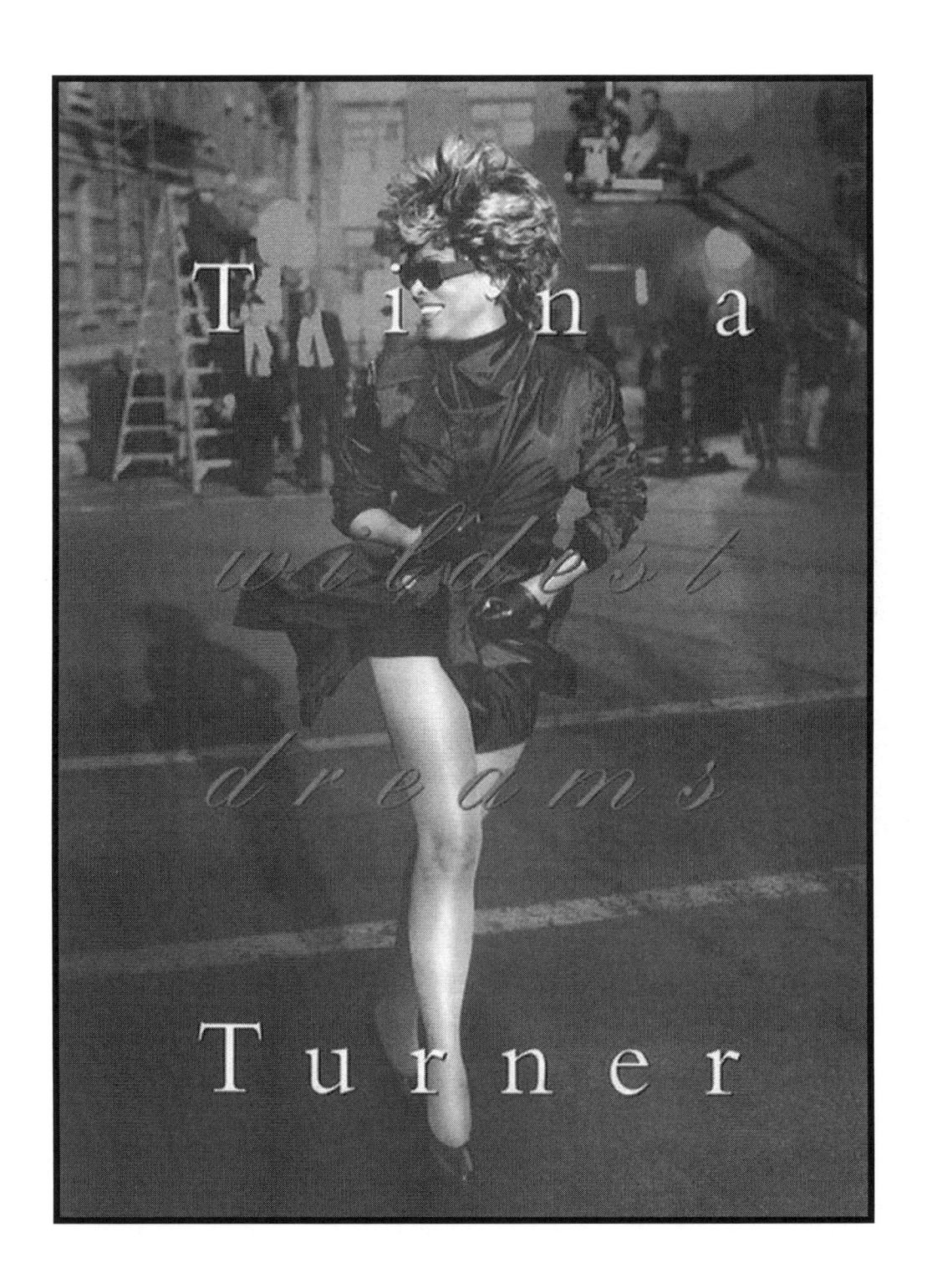

15 ~ **WILDEST DREAMS**

USA/North America: *Missing You (Alternate Mix)/In Your Wildest Dreams* (with Barry White)/*Whatever You Want (Alternate Mix)/Do What You Do/Thief Of Hearts/On Silent Wings/Something Beautiful Remains/Confidential/The Difference Between Us/All Kinds Of People/ Unfinished Sympathy/GoldenEye (Soundtrack Version)/Dancing In My Dreams/Something Beautiful Remains (Joe Urban Remix Edit)*

UK/International: *Do What You Do/Whatever You Want/Missing You/On Silent Wings/ Thief Of Hearts/In Your Wildest Dreams* (with Antonio Banderas)/*GoldenEye (Single Edit)/Confidential/Something Beautiful Remains/All Kinds Of People/Unfinished Sympathy/Dancing In My Dreams/ Something Beautiful Remains (Joe Urban Remix)*

Bonus CD (Special Tour Edition): *In Your Wildest Dreams* (with Barry White)/*Something Beautiful Remains ('Joe' Urban Remix Edit)/The Difference Between Us/River Deep – Mountain High (Live)/ We Don't Need Another Hero (Live)/Private Dancer (Live)/Steamy Windows (Live)/The Best (Live)/On Silent Wings (Live)*

Japan Bonus Track: *Love Is A Beautiful Thing*

Produced by Trevor Horn except *Do What You Do* & *Something Beautiful Remains* by Terry Britten, *GoldenEye* by Bono, The Edge & Nellee Hooper, *Confidential* by Chris Porter & The Pet Shop Boys, *Unfinished Sympathy* by Garry Hughes.

USA: Virgin Records 7243 8 41920 2 0 (1996).

21.09.96: **61**-64-66-78-91

8.03.97: 99-65

UK: Parlophone 7243 8 37684 2 4 (1996), 7243 8 53771 2 9 (Special Tour Edition, 1996).

13.04.96: **4**-8-11-17-19-26-27-29-13-16-11-14-16-14-17-9-7-13-14-18-23-27-34-46-64-59-67-74-51-42-50-64-77-44-40-45-44-39-39-46-49-64-77

Australia
20.05.96: peaked at no.**35**, charted for 16 weeks (Special Tour Edition)

Austria
14.04.96: 6-3-**2**-**2**-4-4-7-11-11-25-23-15-12-6-5-11-11-11-11-12-15-15-19-23-21
15.12.96: 31-21-21-25-28-18-24-34-32-32-39-36-31-37

Belgium
13.04.96: 16-4-**3**-4-5-5-3-3-3-4-4-6-7-11-11-13-16-14-13-10-12-13-12-6-7-10-16-22-21-28-34-x-43-22-17-22-18-13-17-17-17-22-27-30-28-31-33-33

Finland
6.04.96: 9-**3**-**3**-**3**-5-11-12-19-25-31-x-x-x-x-38-35-29-27-13-7-14-17-25

France
1.06.96: **14**-21-21-31-19-25-36
21.09.96: 47
9.11.96: 47-50-36-32-26-26-32

Germany
15.04.96: **2**-**2**-3-3-4-4-9-12-13-13-12-13-11-12-12-12-11-8-8-9-10-16-25-22-25-23-27-30-34-36-45-51-28-26-30-30-32-27-30-29-35-41-79-99-90

Italy
6.04.96: peaked at no.**3**, charted for 15 weeks

Netherlands
13.04.96: 19-8-5-**4**-9-17-22-24-18-18-15-19-22-23-22-27-32-28-34-33-32-30-29-22-12-14-15-16-25-25-32-42-45-38-48-40-42-x-57-54-45-45-49-53-74-71-61-70-67-61

New Zealand
26.05.96: 18-20-23-33 (Special Tour Edition)
23.02.97: 43-33-41-47-36-30-16-10-**1**-**1**-4-10-13-27-x-42-47-45-36-46 (Special Tour Edition)

Norway
8.04.96: 15-**6**-9-13-19-21-27-27-21-22-9-13-15-19-21-34-38-x-36-30-37

Spain
1.04.96: peaked at no.**15**, charted for 14 weeks

Sweden
12.04.96: **5**-6-6-8-10-15-17-13-15-13-11-16-18-14-20-24-21-24-17-17-20-26-37-x-57

Switzerland
14.04.96: **1-1**-2-2-4-5-8-7-10-12-13-13-11-11-10-11-12-8-9-11-11-9-18-20-16-22-25-37-40-x-34

Zimbabwe
10.06.96: peaked at no.**6**

Tina recorded her ninth solo album *WILDEST DREAMS* between the summer of 1995 and early 1996, and it was released outside North America in April 1996.

The album featured guest vocals by Sting on *On Silent Wings* and Neil Tennant of the Pet Shop Boys on *Confidential*, plus a duet with Spanish singer Antonio Banderas, *In Your Wildest Dreams*. Tina re-recorded the latter with Barry White, for the North American edition of the album, which was finally released with a different cover design almost six months later.

Excluding *GoldenEye*, which had been a hit the previous year, *WILDEST DREAMS* produced five hit singles:

- *Whatever You Want*
- *On Silent Wings*
- *Missing You*
- *Something Beautiful Remains*
- *In Your Wildest Dreams* ~ with Barry White

Tina promoted *WILDEST DREAMS* with a massive concert tour, playing 255 dates across five continents, kicking off in Kallang, Singapore on 13th April 1996, and finishing at Hartford, Connecticut, on 10th August 1997.

WILDEST DREAMS went all the way to no.1 in New Zealand and Switzerland, and achieved no.2 in Austria and Germany, no.3 in Belgium, Finland and Italy, no.4 in the Netherlands and the UK, no.5 in Sweden, no.6 in Norway and Zimbabwe, no.14 in France, no.15 in Spain, no.35 in Australia and a disappointing no.61 in the United States.

Special Tour Edition

Outside North America, *WILDEST DREAMS* was reissued ~ using the North American cover art ~ in 1997, with a bonus CD of non-album tracks, remixes and live recordings made during Tina's concerts in Amsterdam, the Netherlands, in early September 1996.

16 ~ VH-1 DIVAS LIVE/99

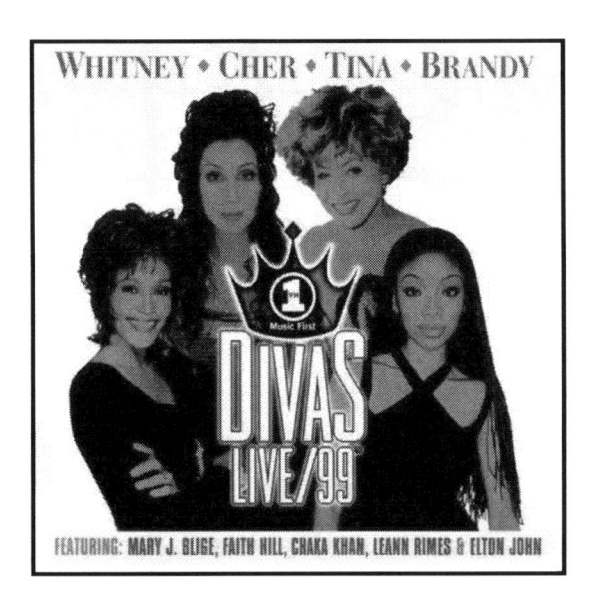

The Best ~ Tina Turner
The Bitch Is Back ~ Tina Turner & Elton John
Proud Mary ~ Tina Turner, Elton John & Cher
If I Could Turn Back Time ~ Cher
How Do I Live ~ LeAnn Rimes
I'm Still Standing ~ Elton John
Have You Ever?/Almost Doesn't Count ~ Brandy
(Everything I Do) I Do It For You ~ Brandy & Faith Hill
This Kiss ~ Faith Hill
Ain't No Way ~ Whitney & Mary J. Blige
I Will Always Love You ~ Whitney
I'm Every Woman ~ Whitney & Chaka Khan
I'm Every Woman (Reprise) ~ Whitney, Chaka Khan, Faith Hill, Brandy, LeAnn Rimes
       & Mary J. Blige

USA: Arista 07822 14604 2 (1999).

20.11.99: **90**

UK: Arista 07822 14604 2 (1999).

VH-1 DIVAS LIVE/99 wasn't a hit in the UK.

Austria
21.11.99: 45-**43**

France
15.01.00: 62-**42**-x-x-62-49-72

Germany
15.11.99: 85-**60**-80-100-66-88-89-89

Netherlands
6.11.99: 83-54-56-64-45-42-**41**-42-42-44-58-77-93

Switzerland
14.11.99: **14**-21-23-31-30-48-64-64-93

The VH-1 Divas Live 2: An Honors Concert For VH1's Save The Music concert was staged at New York's Beacon Theater on 13th April 1999, and was aired live on TV in the United States.

Among the show's presenters were Claudia Schiffer, Elizabeth Hurley and Sarah Michelle Gellar, while celebrity guests in attendance included Donald Trump and Hugh Grant.

During the concert Tina performed:

- *The Best*
- *Let's Stay Together*
- *The Bitch Is Back* ~ with Elton John
- *Proud Mary* ~ with Elton John & Cher

Let's Stay Together was omitted from the *VH-1 DIVAS LIVE/99* album (and accompanying home video), but was later made available via US iTunes.

Despite the impressive line-up, *VH-1 DIVAS LIVE/99* only spent one week on the Top 100 of the Billboard 200, at no.90, in the United States, and failed to chart in the UK. The album performed better in continental Europe, charting at no.14 in Switzerland, no.41 in the Netherlands, no.42 in France, no.43 in Austria and no.60 in Germany.

17 ~ TWENTY FOUR SEVEN

Whatever You Need/All The Woman/When The Heartache Is Over/Absolutely Nothing's Changed/Talk To My Heart/Don't Leave Me This Way/Go Ahead/Without You/Falling/I Will Be There/Twenty Four Seven

Limited Edition Bonus CD (2000): *Twenty Four Seven (Live)/River Deep – Mountain High (Live)/When The Heartache Is Over (Live)/Whatever You Need (Live)/Don't Leave Me This Way (Live)/Talk To My Heart (Live)/Hold On, I'm Coning (Live)/All The Woman (Live)/When The Heartache Is Over (Music Video)/Whatever You Need (Music Video)*

Produced by Terry Bitten except *Whatever You Need, Talk To My Heart & Go Ahead* by Johnny Douglas, *All The Woman & I Will Be There* by Absolute & Johnny Douglas, *Without You* by Absolute, *When The Heartache Is Over & Don't Leave Me This Way* by Brian Rawling & Mark Taylor.

USA: Virgin Records 7243 5 23180 2 5 (2000).

19.02.00: **21**-28-48-60-57-57-44-54-74-89

UK: Parlophone 7243 5 23180 2 5 (1999).

13.11.99: **9**-15-27-31-18-21-23-24-51-60-64-72-80-71-51-64
22.07.00: 15-25-36-49-80

Austria
14.11.99: 6-6-**5**-11-8-17-12-12-16-37-44-43

13.08.00: 30-43

Belgium
13.11.99: 10-11-**9**-**9**-10-10-**9**-11-16-21-22-23-33-39-47

Finland
30.10.99: **6**-16-29-20-22-31-35-37-32
12.08.00: 28

France
6.11.99: **23**-26-42-49-53-59-55-55-71-75
8.07.00: 72

Germany
15.11.99: 4-5-**3**-6-**3**-8-8-19-19-29-34-44-53-56-55-71-86-73-74-85
3.07.00: 95-x-x-72-76-38-42-64-70-88-90-99

Italy
6.11.99: peaked at no.**18**, charted for 8 weeks

Netherlands
6.11.99: 63-26-**24**-40-42-43-44-38-36-49-66-81-91-88-92
29.07.00: 47-38-38-46-60-90

Norway
9.10.99: 6-**5**-6-20-27-25-24-28-25-25-30-21
5.08.00: 32-25-40

Spain
1.11.99: peaked at no.**18**, charted for 6 weeks

Sweden
11.11.99: 11-**6**-9-13-15-23-23-24-36-x-43-38-50-51-x-x-45-46-44-60
10.08.00: 55

Switzerland
14.11.99: **1**-**1**-2-2-2-2-4-7-11-20-31-36-48-49-60-98
9.07.00: 58-43-53-54-61-75

TWENTY FOUR SEVEN is Tina's tenth and final studio album as a solo artist. The album was released in November 1999 in most countries, but it didn't appear until two months later in North America.

Tina did less promotion for *TWENTY FOUR SEVEN* than she had for her previous albums, and this time she didn't promote the album with a tour. Only three singles were released from the album, and only two of them were Top 40 hits:

- *When The Heartache Is Over*
- *Whatever You Need*

The third single, *Don't Leave Me This Way,* was only issued in Europe. It was a minor no.78 hit in Germany, but it failed to chart everywhere else.

TWENTY FOUR SEVEN hit no.1 in Switzerland, no.3 in Germany, no.5 in Austria and Norway, no.6 in Finland and Sweden, no.9 in Belgium and the UK, no.18 in Italy and Spain, no.21 in the United States, no.23 in France and no.24 in the Netherlands.

In 2000, a limited edition of *TWENTY FOUR SEVEN* was released, which came with a bonus CD. The live recordings featured on the CD were recorded during Tina's 60th birthday celebration in London in November 1999. The bonus CD also included the music videos for *When The Heartache Is Over* and *Whatever You Need*.

18 ~ ALL THE BEST

CD1: *Open Arms/Nutbush City Limits/What You Get Is What You See/Missing You/The Best/River Deep – Mountain High/When The Heartache Is Over/Let's Stay Together/I Don't Wanna Fight (7" Edit)/Whatever You Need/I Can't Stand The Rain/GoldenEye (Soundtrack Version)/I Don't Wanna Lose You/Great Spirits/Proud Mary (1993 Version)/Addicted To Love (Live)*

CD2: *In Your Wildest Dreams* (Feat. Antonio Banderas)/*Private Dancer (7" Edit)/Why Must We Wait Until Tonight? (7" Edit)/Typical Male/Tonight/Complicated Disaster/On Silent Wings (Single Edit)/Something Special/We Don't Need Another Hero (Thunderdome) (7" Edit)/It's Only Love/Cose Della Vita/Steamy Windows/Paradise Is Here (7" Edit)/What's Love Got To Do With It/Better Be Good To Me/Two People/Something Beautiful Remains*

USA: Capitol Records CDP 7243 8 63536 2 7 (2005).

19.02.05: **2**-9-27-20-27-31-37-39-67-82-96-99

UK: Parlophone 7243 8 66717 2 1 (2004).

13.11.04: **6**-15-19-21-22-25-25-25-70-68-80-83-x-x-x-x-x-41-68-78
17.03.07: 60-34-47-92
24.04.18: 48-71-72 (*THE GREATEST HITS*)

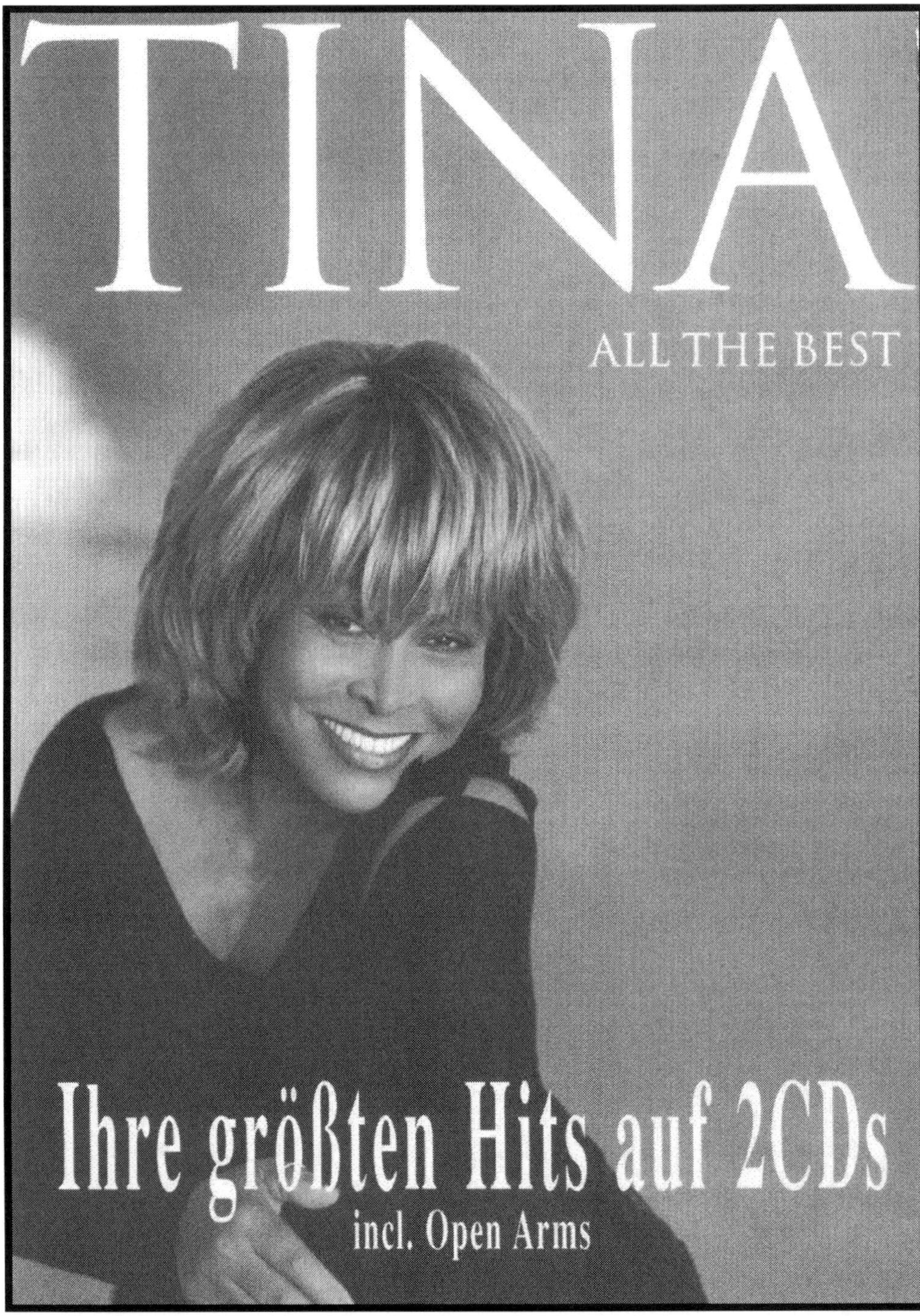
TINA
ALL THE BEST
Ihre größten Hits auf 2CDs
incl. Open Arms

Austria
14.11.04: **3**-7-5-6-7-5-6-6-12-22-29-28-27-25-36-39-49-40-34-42-61-53-67
20.06.14: 33
19.02.16:61-72-67-65-73

Belgium
6.11.04: 55-21-11-11-14-15-9-**5-5-5-5**-6-8-13-12-14-12-16-21-27-25-24-29-34-39-32-31-44-51-69-82-82-93-94-76-82-97-100-x-x-x-93-81

Finland
6.11.04: 33-**15**-17-17-16-28-29-30-37

Germany
15.11.04: **5**-9-10-10-10-10-8-7-12-17-25-31-41-50-45-34-46-33-43-52-56-76-81-80-95-x-86
20.06.14: 64-95

Italy
6.11.04: peaked at no.**8**, charted for 18 weeks

Netherlands
6.11.04: 15-11-26-31-32-35-40-34-46-49-59-41-12-9-**7**-16-23-33-28-39-43-48-53-56-57-83-86-74
6.08.05: 90-52

New Zealand
28.11.04: 23-23-25-23-20-**13**-24-29

Norway
13.11.04: **8**-13-19-23-23-33-40

Spain
9.01.05: 14-**11**-16-20-33-36-39-49-62-68-88-77
23.10.05: 28-52-82-89-75-79
15.01.06: 50-41-33-32-39-38-21-31-60-81-89

Sweden
11.11.04: **14**-18-21-26-30-36-41-50-x-x-46

Switzerland
14.11.04: **3**-3-6-8-7-6-7-4-10-12-14-20-27-29-32-33-43-51-60-78-93-96
15.06.14: 19-46-63
9.10.16: 99
13.01.19: 49

ALL THE BEST is Tina's second international compilation album. It was released in November 2004 in most countries, but North America had to wait until February 2005. Later the same year, in October, an abridged one CD version titled *ALL THE BEST – THE HITS* was also released in North America with the following track listing:

I Don't Wanna Fight (7" Edit)/What's Love Got To Do With It/Proud Mary (1993 Version)/Open Arms/Private Dancer (7" Edit)/The Best/Better Be Good To Me/Let's Stay Together/Nutbush City Limits/Missing You/Complicated Disaster/It's Only Love/Look Me In The Heart/On Silent Wings (Single Edit)/Two People/Typical Male/We Don't Need Another Hero (Thunderdome) (7" Edit)/What You Get Is What You See

Tina recorded three new songs for *ALL THE BEST*:

- *Open Arms*
- *Complicated Disaster*
- *Something Special*

Open Arms and *Complicated Disaster* were both issued as singles, but only *Open Arms* was a hit.

Great Spirits, a Phil Collins penned song Tina had recorded for the 2003 soundtrack album, *BROTHER BEAR*, was also included on *ALL THE BEST*, the first time it had appeared on one of her records.

 ALL THE BEST made its chart debut on the Billboard 200 at no.2, giving Tina her highest chart placing ever on the album chart in the United States. The compilation also achieved no.3 in Austria and Switzerland, no.5 in Belgium and Germany, no.6 in the UK, no.7 in the Netherlands, no.8 in Italy and Norway, no.11 in Spain, no.13 in New Zealand, no.14 in Sweden and no.15 in Finland.

ALL THE BEST was repacked as *THE GREATEST HITS,* and reissued in the UK in 2018, to promote the West End musical, *Tina – The Tina Turner Musical.* The album re-entered the chart at no.48, but climbed no higher during a brief, three week run.

The musical, which was directed by Phyllida Lloyd, premiered at the West End's Aldwych Theatre on 17th April 2018. The following year, on 7th November 2019, the show opened on Broadway. At both venues, Tina was portrayed by Adrienne Warren.

19 ~ TINA!

Steamy Windows/River Deep – Mountain High/Better Be Good To Me/The Acid Queen (Soundtrack Version)/ What You Get Is What You See/What's Love Got To Do With It/Private Dancer (Single Edit)/We Don't Need Another Hero (Thunderdome) (Single Edit)/I Don't Wanna Fight (Single Edit)/GoldenEye (Soundtrack Version)/Let's Stay Together (Live in Amsterdam)/I Can't Stand The Rain (Live in Amsterdam)/Addicted To Love (Live in Camden Palace)/The Best/Proud Mary (1993 Version)/Nutbush City Limits/It Would Be A Crime/I'm Ready

USA: Capitol Records 509992 37422 22 (2008).

18.10.08: **62**-73-96

Europe: Capitol Records 50999 243351 26 (2008).

TINA! released in the UK.

Austria
31.10.08: **13**-16-20-33-44-52-64-52-52-62
13.02.09: 68-28-13-33-44-54

Belgium
18.10.08: 55-28-26-27-27-28-28-32-29-30-32-36-32-42-34-**13**-15-26-23-33-56-64-92-78

Finland
1.05.09: **14**

Germany
31.10.08: **22**-46-44-45-62-68-80-87-81-74-x-x-98-56-79-80-88-x-74-80

Spain
19.10.08: 61-**37**-50-50-56-62-93

Switzerland
26.10.08: **16**-22-29-24-30-38-46-63-77-78-95-98-98-94-79-x-91-34-51-73

This compilation was released to coincide with Tina's 50th Anniversary Tour, which kicked off in Kansas City, Missouri, on 1st October 2008. Tina went on the play 90 dates in North America and Europe, and ended the tour on 5th May 2009 in Sheffield, England.

TINA! was released in North America in September 2008 but, despite Tina touring the United States at the time, the album charted at a lowly no.62.

The following month, the album was issued across continental Europe, and charted at no.13 in Austria and Belgium, no.14 in Finland, no.16 in Switzerland, no.22 in Germany and no.37 in Spain.

20 ~ THE PLATINUM COLLECTION

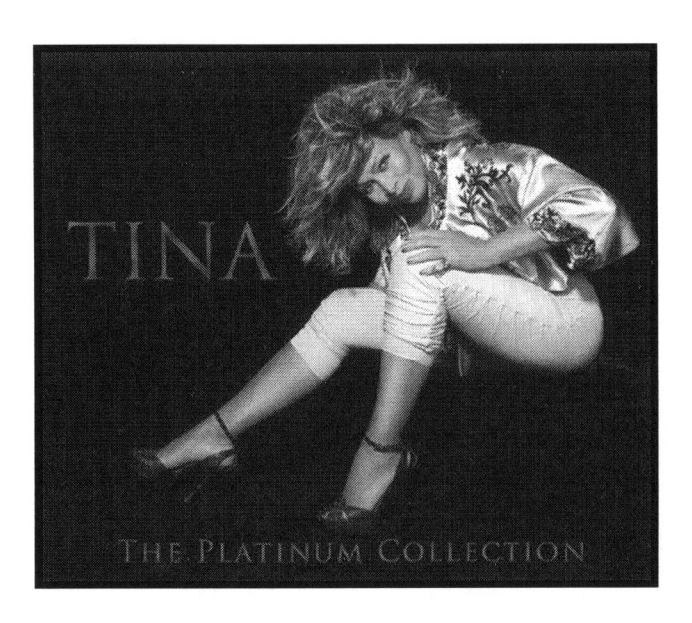

CD1: *What's Love Got To Do With It/Nutbush City Limits/Let's Stay Together/The Acid Queen (Soundtrack Version)/River Deep – Mountain High/Private Dancer (Single Edit)/ Help/Tonight/Better Be Good To Me/ Show Some Respect/I Can't Stand The Rain/It's Only Love/I Want To Take You Higher/ Get Back/Come Together/Proud Mary*

CD2: *The Best/I Don't Wanna Lose You/We Don't Need Another Hero (Thunderdome) (Single Edit)/One Of The Living (Single Edit)/Addicted To Love (Live)/Typical Male/What You Get Is What You See/Tearing Us Apart/Steamy Windows/Two People/Break Every Rule/Look Me In The Heart/Be Tender With Me Baby/Love Thing/Way Of The World/ Nutbush City Limits (The 90's Version)*

CD3: *I Don't Wanna Fight (Single Edit)/It Takes Two/GoldenEye (Soundtrack Version)/I Want You Near Me/Why Must We Wait Until Tonight? (Single Edit)/Whatever You Want/ On Silent Wings (Single Edit)/Missing You/Something Beautiful Remains/In Your Wildest Dreams* (Feat. Antonio Banderas)/*When The Heartache Is Over/Whatever You Need/Open Arms/It Would Be A Crime/I'm Ready/Cose Della Vita*

USA: Not Released.

UK: EMI 50999 2 67097 2 7 (2009).

14.03.09: **14**-25-26-48-51-57-80

Belgium
7.03.09: 70-65-60-74-72-72-77-70-64-56-**36**-72-x-x-x-82

Netherlands
28.02.09: 35-34-20-15-**9**-16-24-25-28-29-27-42-67

In early 2009, to coincide with the European leg of Tina's 50th Anniversary Tour, *TINA!* was expanded from one to three CDs, and issued as *THE PLATINUM COLLECTION* in Europe. The expanded version of the compilation used the same cover photo as *TINA!*, and included most of the hit singles Tina had released as a solo artist, plus several hits she had recorded with Ike.

THE PLATINUM COLLECTION charted at no.9 in the Netherlands, no.14 in the UK and no.36 in Belgium, but coming so soon after *TINA!* it failed to sell in most countries.

21 ~ BUDDHIST AND CHRISTIAN PRAYERS

Beyond/Connecting Hearts (Avalokiteshvara – Blessing Of Swiss Alps)/Sound Of Mystic Law (Lotus Sutra)/Interlude/Holy Praise (Vajra Sattva – Sanctus)/Heavenly Joy (Aithaba – Kyrie Eleison)/Healing Power (Sangye Menhla – Gloria)/Embracing Wisdom (Manjushri – Agnus Dei)/Compassionate Love (Tara – Ave Maria)/Interlude/Purity Of Mind (Lotus Sutra)/Dance With The Divine (Bodhicitta – Halleluja)Power Of Forgiveness (Lotus Sutra – Magnificat – Tara)/Interlude/Devotion (Vajra Guru – Amen)

Produced by Gunther Mende & Mee Eun Kim-Mende.

USA: New Earth Records NE 3107 (2010).

BUDDHIST AND CHRISTIAN PRAYERS wasn't a hit in the United States.

Europe: Decca 4763714 (2009).

BUDDHIST AND CHRISTIAN PRAYERS wasn't a hit in the UK.

Austria
3.07.09: 62-33-26-23-**20**-35-52-69

Germany
3.07.09: 76-**44**-50-66-69-79-91
11.12.09: 85 (Gold Edition)

Switzerland
12.07.09: 8-14-11-22-12-10-**7-7**-17-20-32-52-60-66-88-71-87-87-99-x-x-x-23-38-40-58-64-50-44-62-x-x-x-x-98
14.06.15: 62

Tina became a Buddhist in the early-to-mid 1970s, and she made her home at the Chateau Algonquin, just outside Zurich, Switzerland, in the mid-1990s, eventually applying for and gaining Swiss citizenship.

Tina was invited to be part of the Beyond project by her friend and neighbour, Regula Curti, who was Christian.

'Her mission,' said Tina, 'was to record overlapping and interwoven Christian and Buddhist prayers, and bring them to the people.'

Chanting had been an important part of Tina's life for decades, so she readily agreed, keen to express her spirituality through song. Tina and Regula were joined be another friend and neighbour, Dechen Shak-Dagsay, who was born in Tibet and who, like Tina, was a Buddhist.

The resultant album, *BUDDHIST AND CHRISTIAN PRAYERS*, was released in Switzerland and Germany in 2009, and in North America the following year. The album became a surprise hit, rising to no.7 in Switzerland, no.20 in Austria and no.44 in Germany.

The album failed to enter the Billboard 200 in the United States, but it did chart at no.6 on Billboard's New Age chart.

The success of the album led to an expanded Gold Edition being released, featuring additional Buddhist prayers by Tina. This edition came with a 62 page booklet, printed in English and German.

22 ~ LIVE

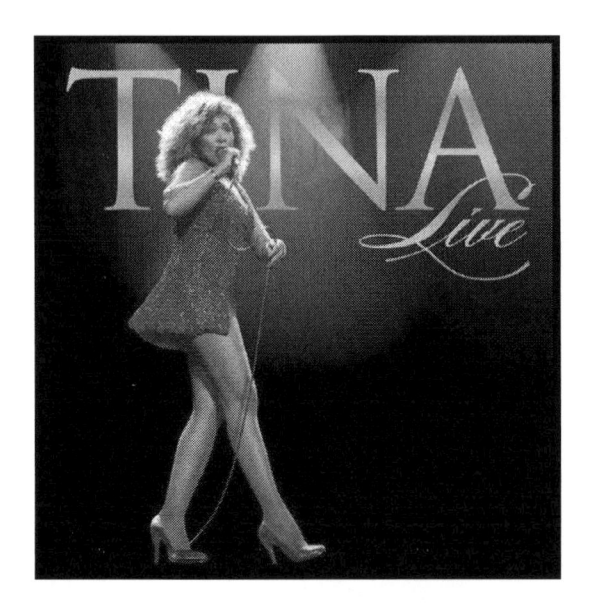

CD: *Steamy Windows/River Deep – Mountain High/What You Get Is What You See/Better Be Good To Me/What's Love Got To Do With It/Private Dancer/We Don't Need Another Hero (Thunderdome)/Let's Stay Together/Jumpin' Jack Flash/It's Only Rock 'N' Roll (But I Like It)* (Feat. Lisa Fischer)/*GoldenEye/Addicted To Love/The Best/Proud Mary/Nutbush City Limits*

DVD: *Introduction Music (Instrumental)/Steamy Windows/Typical Male/River Deep – Mountain High/What You Get Is What You See/Better Be Good To Me/Ninja Chase (Instrumental)/The Acid Queen/What's Love Got To Do With It/What's Love Got To Do With It (Reprise with Audience)/Private Dancer/Weapons Sequence (Instrumental)/We Don't Need Another Hero (Thunderdome)/Help/Let's Stay Together/Undercover Agent For The Blues/I Can't Stand The Rain/Jumpin' Jack Flash/It's Only Rock 'N' Roll (But I Like It)* (Feat. Lisa Fischer)/*Flamenco/009 Encounter (Instrumental)/GoldenEye/Addicted To Love/The Best/Proud Mary/Nutbush City Limits/Be Tender With Me Baby*

USA: Manhattan Records 509996 88531 9 8 (2009).

LIVE wasn't a hit in the United States.

UK: Parlophone 50999 6 88531 2 9 (2009).

10.10.09: **43**

Austria
9.10.09: **8**-23-30-26-51-53-57-61-61

Belgium
3.10.09: 79-**18**-25-29-28-50-74-89

France
3.10.09: **93**

Germany
9.10.09: **18**-41-53-72-x-93
15.01.10: 95

Italy
10.10.09: **36**

Netherlands
3.10.09: **3**-4-4-9-13-26-41-62-64-63-68-68-61-66-69-94-x-99

Spain
11.10.09: **58**-78
5.09.10: 96-65-87

Sweden
9.10.09: **59-59**

Switzerland
11.10.09: 67-68-**58**-74

This live album and accompanying home DVD was recorded during Tina's 50th Anniversary Tour, at the GelreDome in Arnhem, the Netherlands, on 21st March 2009. During the concert, as well as her own hits, Tina performed two Rolling Stones hits, *Jumpin' Jack Flash* and *It's Only Rock'N'Roll (But I Like It)*.

Tina's performance of *It's Only Rock 'N' Roll (But I Like It)* featured Lisa Fischer.

The CD/DVD were released together as a double pack, but whereas the DVD featured the entire concert, the CD only featured select highlights.

LIVE sold best in the Netherlands, where the album was recorded, and peaked at no.3. Elsewhere, the album charted at no.8 in Austria, no.18 in Belgium and Germany, no.36 in Italy, no.43 in the UK, no.58 in Spain and Switzerland, and no.59 in Sweden.

23 ~ CHILDREN – WITH CHILDREN UNITED IN PRAYER

Calling By Tina/Om Am Hum/Allah Hu/Kol Ha' Olam Kulo/Halleluja/Sa Ta Na Ma/ Ganesha Sharanam/Buddham Saranam Gaccami/Jai Da Da/Sallallah' Al Muhammad/ Veni Sancte Spiritus/Ra Ma Da Sa/Sarvesham Svastir Bhavatu/Unity

Produced by Roland Frei.

Switzerland: Universal Music 278 143-1 (2011).

23.10.11: **21**-32-38-46-**21**-**21**-29-68-76-27-24-30-46-53-52-52-68-67-74

Germany
28.10.11: **78**-79-99-x-94

The second album in the Beyond project featured prayers and mantras from six different religions: Buddhism, Christianity, Judaism, Islam, Hinduism and Sikhism. On the album, Tina, Regula Curti and Dechen Shak-Dagsay were joined by a choir of 30 children from different cultural and religious backgrounds.

To promote *CHILDREN – WITH CHILDREN UNITED IN PRAYER*, the three members of Beyond, together with the children, appeared on TV shows in Germany and Switzerland. At the same time *Unity*, the final track on the album, was issued as a digital single but it wasn't a hit anywhere.

Tina also appeared on the April 2013 German issue of *Vogue* magazine ~ at 73, she was the oldest person ever to feature on the cover of any *Vogue* magazine, anywhere in the world.

VOGUE
DEUTSCH

4/2013
APRIL
€ 6,-
DEUTSCHLAND
€ 8,- ÖSTERREICH
SFR 10,- SCHWEIZ

„Ein Comeback?
Dazu muss ich
mich erst neu erfinden."
Tina Turner

Simply
the best!

MODE-MAGIE
VON JEANS BIS HAUTE COUTURE

STIL-IKONEN
JIL SANDER, MANOLO BLAHNIK,
IRIS BERBEN IM INTERVIEW

CHILDREN – WITH CHILDREN UNITED IN PRAYER charted at no.21 in Switzerland and no.78 in Germany.

All the proceeds from the album were donated, in equal amounts, to three charities: The Tina Foundation, The Seechau Foundation and The Dewa Che Foundation.

In 2016, *CHILDREN – WITH CHILDREN UNITED IN PRAYER* was repackaged and reissued, and served as the soundtrack to the animated film, *Planting Seeds Of Mindfulness*, in which Jasper, a 16 year old Asian-African-American boy uses the power of mindfulness, meditation and kindness to cope with everyday family and school life.

24 ~ LOVE SONGS

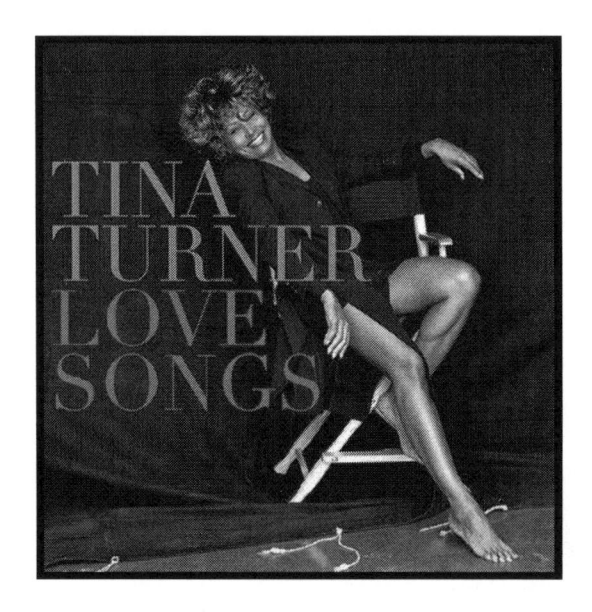

The Best (Edit)/I Don't Wanna Lose You/Let's Stay Together (Single Version)/What's Love Got To Do With It/Missing You (Single Edit)/Private Dancer (Single Edit)/Two People/Look Me In The Heart/Way Of The World/ Why Must We Wait Until Tonight? (7" Edit)/Falling/I Want You Near Me/Be Tender With Me Baby/Don't Leave Me This Way/I Don't Wanna Fight (Single Edit)/Whatever You Need (Edit)/When The Heartache Is Over/River Deep – Mountain High

USA: Parlophone RP2-54193 (2014).

LOVE SONGS wasn't a hit in the USA.

UK: Parlophone 2564633791 (2014).

15.02.14: 32-**30**-63-77

Germany
28.02.14: **56**
20.06.14: 90-67

Spain
9.02.14: **88**-94

Switzerland
23.02.14: **30**-55-62

This compilation of 18 love songs was released to coincide with Valentine's Day.

LOVE SONGS was only a modest hit, faring best in Switzerland and the UK, where it achieved no.30. The compilation also charted at no.56 in Germany, and was a minor hit in Spain, but it failed to chart in many countries, including the United States.

25 ~ LOVE WITHIN

Love Within/Wisdom/Almighty/Divine Mother/Praise/Mother Within/Welcome/Lover Beyond/Compassion/Oneness

Produced by Roland Frei.

USA & UK: Not Released.

Switzerland: Panorama 4793344 (2014).

15.06.14: 9-**7**-10-13-16-26-45-55-80-49-64-54-95-74

Austria
20.06.14: **38**-74-54-74-64

Germany
20.06.14: 28-25-**21-21**-23-38-92-x-x-40-49-73-91-61-92

On *LOVE WITHIN*, the third album in the Beyond project, Tina, Regula Curti and Dechen Shak-Dagsay were joined by a fourth member, Hindu singer Sawani Shende-Sathaye.
   Two digital singles were released to promote the album.
   The first, titled *Mother*, was actually an edited version of the track *Wisdom*. It was released to coincide with Mother's Day, and carried the message 'Dedicated to all the wonderful mothers of the world. Happy Mothers Day from Tina, Regula, Dechen and Sawani.

The second digital single, *Heavenly Home*, was an edited, more up-tempo version of *Mother Within*.

LOVE WITHIN charted at no.7 in Switzerland, no.21 in Germany and no.38 in Austria.

26 ~ AWAKENING

CD1: *Rain Songs/Be Now In Your Hands/Salutations/Partos Trocados/Avalokiteshvara/ Wiegenlied/Nini Nini/Sojaa Sojaa*

CD2: *Mountain Blessing/Lama Chenno/One Soul/Two Loves/Caritas Abundat/Awakening Beyond (Part 1)/Awakening Beyond (Part 2)/ Awakening Beyond (Part 3)*

Produced by Kareem Roustom.

USA & UK : Not Released.

Europe: iGroove Music 222629 (2017).

Switzerland
19.11.17: **15**

AWAKENING, which was released as a double CD, was the fourth and final album by the Beyond project.
    The album was recorded by six female singers from six different cultures. With Dechen Shak-Dagsay having left the project, Tina, Regula Curti and Sawani Shende-Sathaye were joined by Ani Choying Drolma (from Nepal), Dima Orsho (Syria) and Mor Karbasi (Israel).
    AWAKENING was recorded at London's Abbey Road studios with the London Philharmonic Orchestra.
    Tina only contributed to two titles to the album:

- *Rain Songs* ~ with Sawanai Shende & Dima Orsho.
- *Awakening Beyond (Part 1)* ~ with Mor Karbasi, Dima Orsho & Ani Choying Drolma.

AWAKENING charted at no.15 in Switzerland, but it wasn't a hit anywhere else.

In November 2018, the four Beyond albums were released together as deluxe editions in hardcover books, as a box-set titled *COLLECTOR'S BOX*.

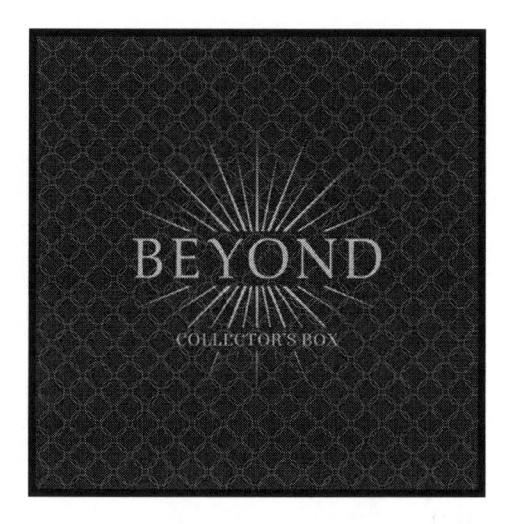

The release of *COLLECTOR'S BOX* was timed to coincide with the publication of Tina's autobiography, *My Love Story*.

THE ALMOST TOP 40 ALBUMS

Two of Tina's albums, one with Ike, have made the Top 50 in one or more countries, but failed to enter the Top 40 in any.

SWEET RHODE ISLAND RED

This 1974 album by Ike & Tina Turner rose to no.41 in Australia in early 1975, one place short of Top 40 status, and spent 14 weeks on the chart. But, like the title track as a single, it failed to enter the Top 40 anywhere.

PRIVATE DANCER MIXES

This mini-album, released a year after the hugely successful *PRIVATE DANCER*, featured three 'Dance Mixes' and three 'Rock Mixes'. The album was exclusively released in Australasia and Japan, where it charted at no.64 in Australia and no.41 in New Zealand ~ again, just one place shy of Top 40 status.

TINA'S TOP 20 ALBUMS

This Top 20 has been compiled using the same points system as for the Tina's Top 40 Singles listing.

Rank/Album/Points

1 *FOREIGN AFFAIR* – 2164 points

2 *PRIVATE DANCER* – 1996 points

3 *SIMPLY THE BEST* – 1939 points

Rank/Album/Points

4 *BREAK EVERY RULE* – 1789 points

5 *WILDEST DREAMS* – 1681 points

6. *WHAT'S LOVE GOT TO DO WITH IT* – 1366 points
7. *ALL THE BEST* – 1274 points
8. *TWENTY FOUR SEVEN* – 1173 points
9. *LIVE IN EUROPE* – 873 points
10. *MAD MAX BEYOND THUNDERDOME* – 584 points

11. *LIVE* – 529 points
12. *TINA!* – 491 points
13. *NUTBUSH CITY LIMITS* – 445 points
14. *VH-1 DIVAS LIVE/99* – 262 points
15. *THE PLATINUM COLLECTION* – 228 points

16. *LOVE WITHIN* – 217 points
17. *WORKIN' TOGETHER* – 176 points
18. *LOVE SONGS* – 167 points
19. *WHAT YOU HEAR IS WHAT YOU GET* – 146 points
20. *TINA LIVE* – 125 points

Although *PRIVATE DANCER* is her best-selling album, *FOREIGN AFFAIR* emerges as Tina's most successful album in terms of chart success. Her most successful compilation, *SIMPLY THE BEST*, is at no.3, with *BREAK EVERY RULE* and *WILDEST DREAMS* completing the Top 5. Two albums by Ike & Tina feature in the Top 20, with *NUTBUSH CITY LIMITS* at no.13 and *WORKIN' TOGETHER* at no.17.

Tina's most recent Top 40 album, *LOVE WITHIN* with the Beyond project, makes an appearance at no.16.

ALBUMS TRIVIA

To date, Tina has achieved twenty-six Top 40 albums in one or more of the countries featured in this book, including six albums credited to Ike & Tina Turner and four with the Beyond project.

There follows a country-by-country look at Tina's most successful albums, starting with her homeland.

TINA IN THE USA

Tina has achieved 14 hit albums in the United States, which spent 245 weeks on the Top 100 of the Billboard 200 chart.

Her highest charting album is *ALL THE BEST*, which peaked at no.2.

Albums with the most weeks

84 weeks	*PRIVATE DANCER*
39 weeks	*BREAK EVERY RULE*
19 weeks	*WORKIN' TOGETHER*
18 weeks	*WHAT YOU HEAR IS WHAT YOU GET – LIVE AT CARNEGIE HALL*
17 weeks	*FOREIGN AFFAIR*
17 weeks	*WHAT'S LOVE GOT TO DO WITH IT*
12 weeks	*ALL THE BEST*
10 weeks	*MAD MAX BEYOND THUNDERDOME*
10 weeks	*TWENTY FOUR SEVEN*

RIAA (Recording Industry Association of America) Awards

The RIAA began certifying Gold albums in 1958, Platinum albums in 1976, and multi-Platinum albums in 1984. Gold = 500,000, Platinum = 1 million. Awards are based on shipments, not sales, and each disc is counted individually (so, for example, a double album has to ship 500,000 to be eligible for Platinum).

5 x Platinum	*PRIVATE DANCER* (September 1987) = 5 million
Platinum	*BREAK EVERY RULE* (November 1986) = 1 million
Platinum	*SIMPLY THE BEST* (November 1994) = 1 million
Platinum	*WHAT'S LOVE GOT TO DO WITH IT* (November 1994) = 1 million
Platinum	*ALL THE BEST* (March 2005) = 1 million
Gold	*WHAT YOU HEAR IS WHAT YOU GET* (September 1972) = 500,000

Gold   *FOREIGN AFFAIR* (November 1989) = 500,000
Gold   *TWENTY FOUR SEVEN* (March 2000) = 500,000

TINA IN AUSTRALIA

Tina has achieved 16 hit albums in Australia, which spent 393 weeks on the chart.

Her most successful album is *PRIVATE DANCER*, which peaked at no.7.

Albums with the most weeks

77 weeks	*SIMPLY THE BEST*
74 weeks	*PRIVATE DANCER*
46 weeks	*NUTBUSH CITY LIMITS*
46 weeks	*FOREIGN AFFAIR*
38 weeks	*BREAK EVERY RULE*
17 weeks	*WHAT'S LOVE GOT TO DO WITH IT*
16 weeks	*WILDEST DREAMS*
14 weeks	*SWEET RHODE ISLAND RED*
13 weeks	*MAD MAX BEYOND THUNDERDOME*
12 weeks	*ACID QUEEN*

TINA IN AUSTRIA

Tina has achieved 16 hit albums in Austria, which spent 366 weeks on the chart.

No.1 Albums

1985	*PRIVATE DANCER*
1989	*FOREIGN AFFAIR*

Most weeks at No.1

8 weeks	*FOREIGN AFFAIR*
6 weeks	*PRIVATE DANCER*

Albums with the most weeks

56 weeks	*PRIVATE DANCER*
53 weeks	*FOREIGN AFFAIR*
50 weeks	*BREAK EVERY RULE*
39 weeks	*WILDEST DREAMS*

29 weeks	*ALL THE BEST*
28 weeks	*SIMPLY THE BEST*
18 weeks	*LIVE IN EUROPE*
18 weeks	*WHAT'S LOVE GOT TO DO WITH IT*
15 weeks	*TINA!*
14 weeks	*TWENTY FOUR SEVEN*

TINA IN BELGIUM (Flanders)

Since 1995, Tina has achieved seven hit albums in Belgium (Flanders), which spent 168 weeks on the chart.

Her most successful album is *WILDEST DREAMS*, which peaked at no.3.

Albums with the most weeks

47 weeks	*WILDEST DREAMS*
40 weeks	*ALL THE BEST*
24 weeks	*TINA!*
21 weeks	*SIMPLY THE BEST*
15 weeks	*TWENTY FOUR SEVEN*
13 weeks	*THE PLATINUM COLLECTION*

Note: no information is available on the Belgian album chart pre-1995.

TINA IN FINLAND

Tina has achieved five hit albums in Finland, which spent 43 weeks on the chart.

Her most successful album is *WILDEST DREAMS*, which peaked at no.3.

Albums with the most weeks

19 weeks	*WILDEST DREAMS*
10 weeks	*TWENTY FOUR SEVEN*
9 weeks	*ALL THE BEST*

TINA IN FRANCE

Tina has achieved seven hit albums in France, which spent 92 weeks on the chart.

Her most successful album is *WILDEST DREAMS*, which peaked at no14.

Albums with the most weeks

32 weeks	*FOREIGN AFFAIR*
20 weeks	*WHAT'S LOVE GOT TO DO WITH IT*
15 weeks	*WILDEST DREAMS*
11 weeks	*TWENTY FOUR SEVEN*
8 weeks	*BREAK EVERY RULE*

TINA IN GERMANY

Tina has achieved 20 hit albums in Germany, which spent 536 weeks on the chart.

No.1 Albums

1986	*BREAK EVERY RULE*
1989	*FOREIGN AFFAIR*

Most weeks at No.1

9 weeks	*BREAK EVERY RULE*
4 weeks	*FOREIGN AFFAIR*

Albums with the most weeks

94 weeks	*PRIVATE DANCER*
64 weeks	*FOREIGN AFFAIR*
60 weeks	*BREAK EVERY RULE*
51 weeks	*SIMPLY THE BEST*
45 weeks	*WILDEST DREAMS*
31 weeks	*TWENTY FOUR SEVEN*
28 weeks	*ALL THE BEST*
23 weeks	*WHAT'S LOVE GOT TO DO WITH IT*
20 weeks	*WORKIN' TOGETHER*
19 weeks	*LIVE IN EUROPE*

TINA IN ITALY

Tina has achieved 11 hit albums in Italy, which spent 154 weeks on the chart.

Her most successful album is *FOREIGN AFFAIR*, which peaked at no.2.

Albums with the most weeks

35 weeks	*FOREIGN AFFAIR*
20 weeks	*WHAT'S LOVE GOT TO DO WITH IT*
19 weeks	*SIMPLY THE BEST*
18 weeks	*ALL THE BEST*
15 weeks	*WILDEST DREAMS*
14 weeks	*BREAK EVERY RULE*
13 weeks	*NUTBUSH CITY LIMITS*

TINA IN JAPAN

Tina has achieved six hit albums in Japan, which spent 35 weeks on the chart.

Her most successful album is *GOLD DISC*, which peaked at no.22.

Albums with the most weeks

10 weeks	*GOLD DISC*
9 weeks	*BREAK EVERY RULE*
8 weeks	*PRIVATE DANCER*

TINA IN THE NETHERLANDS

Tina has achieved 13 hit albums in the Netherlands, which spent 438 weeks on the chart.

Her highest charting albums are *PRIVATE DANCER* and *LIVE*, which both peaked at no.3.

Albums with the most weeks

83 weeks	*SIMPLY THE BEST*
67 weeks	*PRIVATE DANCER*
51 weeks	*FOREIGN AFFAIR*
49 weeks	*WILDEST DREAMS*
36 weeks	*BREAK EVERY RULE*
31 weeks	*LIVE IN EUROPE*
30 weeks	*ALL THE BEST*
27 weeks	*WHAT'S LOVE GOT TO DO WITH IT*
21 weeks	*TWENTY FOUR SEVEN*
17 weeks	*LIVE*

TINA IN NEW ZEALAND

Tina has achieved 10 hit albums in New Zealand, which spent 280 weeks on the chart.

No.1 Albums

1991	*SIMPLY THE BEST*
1997	*WILDEST DREAMS* (Special Tour Edition)

Both albums topped the chart for two weeks.

Albums with the most weeks

91 weeks	*SIMPLY THE BEST*
75 weeks	*PRIVATE DANCER*
26 weeks	*BREAK EVERY RULE*
26 weeks	*WHAT'S LOVE GOT TO DO WITH IT*
23 weeks	*WILDEST DREAMS*
19 weeks	*FOREIGN AFFAIR*

TINA IN NORWAY

Tina has achieved nine hit albums in Norway, which spent 127 weeks on the chart.

No.1 Albums

1989 *FOREIGN AFFAIR*

FOREIGN AFFAIR topped the chart for three weeks.

Albums with the most weeks

25 weeks	*SIMPLY THE BEST*
21 weeks	*FOREIGN AFFAIR*
20 weeks	*WILDEST DREAMS*
15 weeks	*TWENTY FOUR SEVEN*
13 weeks	*BREAK EVERY RULE*
10 weeks	*PRIVATE DANCER*

TINA IN SOUTH AFRICA

Tina has achieved five hit albums in Spain, which spent 80 weeks on the chart.

No.1 Albums

1989   *FOREIGN AFFAIR*
1991   *SIMPLY THE BEST*

Most weeks at No.1

10 weeks   *FOREIGN AFFAIR*
 4 weeks   *SIMPLY THE BEST*

Albums with the most weeks

32 weeks   *FOREIGN AFFAIR*
29 weeks   *SIMPLY THE BEST*
15 weeks   *PRIVATE DANCER*

TINA IN SPAIN

Tina has achieved 14 hit albums in Spain, which spent 246 weeks on the chart.

No.1 Albums

1986   *BREAK EVERY RULE*

BREAK EVERY RULE topped the chart for three weeks.

Albums with the most weeks

37 weeks   *PRIVATE DANCER*
37 weeks   *BREAK EVERY RULE*
30 weeks   *FOREIGN AFFAIR*
29 weeks   *ALL THE BEST*
26 weeks   *SIMPLY THE BEST*
20 weeks   *WHAT'S LOVE GOT TO DO WITH IT*
14 weeks   *LIVE IN EUROPE*
14 weeks   *WILDEST DREAMS*
11 weeks   *MAD MAX BEYOND THUNDERDOME*

TINA IN SWEDEN

Tina has achieved 10 hit albums in Sweden, which spent 185 weeks on the chart.

No.1 Albums

1989   FOREIGN AFFAIR

FOREIGN AFFAIR topped the chart for four weeks.

Albums with the most weeks

32 weeks	PRIVATE DANCER
30 weeks	FOREIGN AFFAIR
24 weeks	SIMPLY THE BEST
24 weeks	WILDEST DREAMS
23 weeks	WHAT'S LOVE GOT TO DO WITH IT
22 weeks	BREAK EVERY RULE
18 weeks	TWENTY FOUR SEVEN
10 weeks	LIVE IN EUROPE

TINA IN SWITZERLAND

Tina has achieved 18 hit albums in Switzerland, which spent 420 weeks on the chart.

No.1 Albums

1986	BREAK EVERY RULE
1989	FOREIGN AFFAIR
1996	WILDEST DREAMS
1999	TWENTY FOUR SEVEN

Most weeks at No.1

10 weeks	FOREIGN AFFAIR
2 weeks	BREAK EVERY RULE
2 weeks	WILDEST DREAMS
2 weeks	TWENTY FOUR SEVEN

Albums with the most weeks

88 weeks	PRIVATE DANCER
51 weeks	FOREIGN AFFAIR
40 weeks	BREAK EVERY RULE
30 weeks	WILDEST DREAMS
29 weeks	BUDDHIST AND CHRISTIAN PRAYERS
27 weeks	ALL THE BEST

26 weeks   *WHAT'S LOVE GOT TO DO WITH IT*
23 weeks   *SIMPLY THE BEST*
23 weeks   *TWENTY FOUR SEVEN*
19 weeks   *TINA!*
19 weeks   *CHILDREN – WITH CHILDREN UNITED IN PRAYER*

TINA IN THE UK

Tina has achieved 14 hit albums in the UK, which spent 624 weeks on the chart.

No.1 Albums

1989   *FOREIGN AFFAIR*
1993   *WHAT'S LOVE GOT TO DO WITH IT*

Both albums topped the chart for one week.

Albums with the most Top 100 weeks

198 weeks   *SIMPLY THE BEST*
150 weeks   *PRIVATE DANCER*
 81 weeks   *FOREIGN AFFAIR*
 49 weeks   *BREAK EVERY RULE*
 43 weeks   *WILDEST DREAMS*
 34 weeks   *WHAT'S LOVE GOT TO DO WITH IT*
 22 weeks   *ALL THE BEST / THE GRESTEST HITS*
 21 weeks   *TWENTY FOUR SEVEN*
 13 weeks   *LIVE IN EUROPE*

The Brit Certified/BPI (British Phonographic Industry) Awards

The BPI began certifying albums in 1973, and between April 1973 and December 1978, awards related to a monetary value and not a unit value. Thanks to inflation, this changed several times over the years:

- April 1973 – August 1974: Silver = £75,000, Gold = £150,000, Platinum = £1 million.
- September 1974 – December 1975: Gold raised to £250,000, others unchanged.
- January 1976 – December 1976: Silver raised to £100,000, others unchanged.
- January 1977 – December 1978: Silver raised to £150,000, Gold raised to £300,000, Platinum unchanged.

When this system was abolished, the awards that were set remain in place today: Silver = 60,000, Gold = 100,000, Platinum = 300,000. Multi-Platinum awards were introduced in February 1987.

In July 2013 the BPI automated awards, and awards from this date are based on actual sales since February 1994, not shipments.

8 x Platinum	*SIMPLY THE BEST* (March 2000)	= 2.4 million
5 x Platinum	*FOREIGN AFFAIR* (August 1991)	= 1.5 million
3 x Platinum	*PRIVATE DANCER* (June 1986)	= 900,000
2 x Platinum	*WILDEST DREAMS* (March 2000)	= 600,000
Platinum	*BREAK EVERY RULE* (March 1987)	= 300,000
Platinum	*WHAT'S LOVE GOT TO DO WITH IT* (December 1993)	= 300,000
Platinum	*TWENTY FOUR SEVEN* (December 1999)	= 300,000
Platinum	*ALL THE BEST* (December 2004)	= 300,000
Gold	*LIVE IN EUROPE* (April 1988)	= 100,000
Gold	*THE PLATINUM COLLECTION* (December 2018)	= 100,000

TINA IN ZIMBABWE

Tina has achieved five hit albums in Zimbabwe.

Her most successful album is *PRIVATE DANCER*, which peaked at no.2.

Note: the number of weeks each album spent on the chart is unknown.